# *Understanding Cultural Diversity*

American Correctional Association

Perry M. Johnson, President
James A. Gondles, Jr., Executive Director
Linda H. Munday, Acting Director of Communications
and Publications
Elizabeth Watts, Publications Managing Editor
Marianna Nunan, Project Editor
Jennifer A. Nichols, Production Editor
Cover design by Elinor Allen

ISBN 0-929310-93-4

Printed in the United States of America by BookCrafters,
Fredericksburg, Va.

This publication may be ordered from:
American Correctional Association
8025 Laurel Lakes Court
Laurel, MD 20707-5075
1-800-825-BOOK

# Contents

# Foreword

Cultural diversity has been around a long time, though we have perhaps not realized it. The old idea of the United States as a "melting pot" of different cultures all combining to form one has given way to a new idea of a cultural "salad" or "quilt": one where cultures still maintain their unique qualities and combine to form a larger, richer whole.

Recognizing cultural diversity is a positive step forward for corrections and the nation. A reflection of our ever-shrinking world, multiculturalism will be with us into the next century. As Elliott Caggins puts it in his introduction to this book, "There are more similarities than there are differences among people around the world. If the similarities are emphasized and the differences are accepted, much of the difficulties arising from cultural diversity can be overcome." It is hoped that *Understanding Cultural Diversity* can assist in this process.

*James A. Gondles, Jr.*
*Executive Director*

# 1. Multiculturalism in Corrections: Perceptions and Awareness

*By Elliott Caggins*

Correctional agencies need to have a global perspective of multiculturalism to flourish in the 1990s and beyond. To have a global perspective means to consider the likelihood that corrections will have to accommodate offenders from a multitude of cultures.

The chapters in *Understanding Cultural Diversity* aim to increase cultural awareness and to promote multiculturalism in the correctional workplace.

People are different from each other because they share different backgrounds, which are their personal experiences, beliefs, training, education, religion, and value systems. There are, however, more similarities than there are differences among people around the world. If the similarities are emphasized and the differences are accepted, much of the difficulties arising from cultural diversity can be overcome.

The clear and driving force throughout this book is the desire to understand and explicate the nature of interpersonal communication as it affects and is affected by a multicultural environment. Interpersonal communication seen from this perspective is an element of group identification that manifests itself in the verbal and/or nonverbal messages exchanged.

This book synthesizes a culturally diverse and complex literature for correctional workers. For example, the ability to understand the influence of culture on communication is dependent on the ability to

*Elliott Caggins is program development manager for the Bureau of Prisons Staff Training Academy in Glynco, Georgia.*

understand a myriad of studies that profess to identify basic dimensions along which cultures vary.

Many of the authors of the chapters that follow are correctional practitioners, and their views are based on their life experiences. They have an understanding of the historical roots of the culture discussed, the differences among groups within that culture, and the various aspects of that culture (philosophy, values, traditions, and holidays).

# What Is Culture?

Culture is a distinctly human capacity for adapting to circumstances and transmitting this coping skill and knowledge to future generations. Culture gives people a sense of who they are, of belonging, of how they should behave, and of what they should be doing.

Having a sense of culture and its related skills are unique human attributes. Culture includes problem-solving tools for daily coping in a particular environment. It enables people to create a distinctive world around themselves, to control their own destinies, and to grow in self-esteem. Culture gives people a sense of identity, especially in terms of human behavior and appropriate values. Culture provides insight into people. Therefore, everyone benefits from understanding both the generalizations and specifics of a culture. This understanding facilitates intercultural communication and good, sound working relations.

# Characteristics of Culture

Culture provides people with a sense of identity through its characteristics, such as its values and norms, beliefs and attitudes, relationships, communication and language, sense of self and space, appearance and dress, work habits and practices, and food and eating habits.

## *Values and Norms*

The need systems of cultures vary, as do the priorities they attach to certain behavior in the group. Those operating on a survival level value the gathering of food, adequate covering, and shelter. Those with high security needs value material things, money, job titles, as well as law and order.

*Values* are fundamental beliefs about behavior, customs, and institutions that are judged either favorably or unfavorably by a people, ethnic groups, or society.

*Norms* are commonly held standards that define acceptable and unacceptable behavior of individuals within a group. Norms are almost always culture-specific, and they vary widely from one cultural environment to another.

Although they are unwritten, norms are widely known by group members. These rules are communicated informally, through interactions with family, friends, and co-workers. Individuals may not think much about the norms they have grown up with, but they quickly recognize those who share their norms—those who play by the same social rules—and those who do not.

The United States is in the midst of a values revolution as the children of the depression days give way to the children of affluence who have different values, like the quality of life, self-fulfillment, and meaning in experiences. In some Pacific Island cultures, the greater one's status becomes, the more one is expected to give away or share.

Through its value system, a culture sets the norms of behavior for its society. These acceptable standards for membership may range from the work ethic or pleasure to absolute obedience or permissiveness for children or from rigid submission of a wife to her husband to the total liberation of women.

According to anthropologist Ina Brown (Harris & Moran 1991), people in different cultures are pleased, concerned, annoyed, or embarrassed about different things because they perceive situations in terms of different sets of premises. Because conventions are learned, some cultures demand honesty among members of one's own group, but accept a more relaxed standard with strangers. Some of these conventions are expressed in gift giving; rituals of birth, death, and marriage; and guidelines for privacy, showing respect or deference, and expressing good manners.

## Beliefs and Attitudes

It is difficult to determine the major beliefs of a people and how these beliefs and other factors influence their attitudes toward themselves, others, and their lifestyles. Attitudes are the tendencies of an individual to respond to certain situations in one way rather than another. People in all cultures seem to have a concern for the supernatural evident in their religions and religious practices.

## Relationships

Cultures fix human and organizational relationships by age, sex, status, and degree of kindred, as well as by wealth, power, and wisdom. The family unit is the most common expression of this characteristic, and the arrangement may range from small to large. In some cultures, the authoritarian figure in the family is the head male. This fixed relationship is often extended from home to community, explaining some societies' preference for a dictator who leads the national family. Relationships between and among people vary by category. In some cultures the elderly are honored, whereas in others they are ignored. In some cultures women must wear veils and appear deferential, while in others women are considered equal, if not superior to men.

## Communication and Language

A group's communication system, verbal and nonverbal, distinguishes it from another group. Some nations have fifteen or more major spoken languages, and within one language group there may be many dialects, accents, slang, jargon, and other such variations. Furthermore, the meanings given to gestures often differ by culture. So although body language may be universal, its manifestation differs by locality.

## Sense of Self and Space

Self-identity and appreciation can be manifested by humble bearing in one culture, while another culture calls for macho behavior. Independence and creativity are countered in other cultures by group cooperation and conformity. Representatives of some cultures, such as Americans, have a sense of space that requires more physical distance between an individual and others. Latins and Vietnamese tend to get much closer. Some cultures are very structured and formal, while others are flexible and informal. Some cultures are closed and determine one's place precisely, while others are open and changing. Each culture validates self in a unique way.

### Appearance and Dress

Appearance and dress include outward garments and adornments, or lack thereof, as well as body decorations that tend to be culturally distinct. The Japanese kimono, the African headdress, the Englishman's bowler and umbrella, the Polynesian sarong, and the American Indian headband are all distinct to their cultures. Some cultures smear their faces for battle, while others use cosmetics to manifest beauty.

### Work Habits and Practices

Another dimension of a group's culture is its attitudes toward work, the dominant types of work, the division of work, and work habits or practices, such as promotions or rewards. Work is defined as exertion or effort directed to produce or accomplish something. Some cultures espouse a work ethic in which all members are expected to engage in a desirable and worthwhile activity.

### Food and Eating Habits

The manner in which food is selected, prepared, presented, and eaten often differs by culture. One person's pet is another person's delicacy. Americans love beef, yet it is forbidden to Hindus. The forbidden food for Moslems and Jews is normally pork, which is eaten extensively by the Chinese and others. In large cosmopolitan cities, restaurants often cater to diverse diets and offer "national" dishes to satisfy varying cultural tastes. Eating habits also differ, ranging from hands and chopsticks to full sets of cutlery. Even when cultures use the same utensil, such as a fork, a European can often be distinguished from an American by which hand he or she uses to hold the implement.

# Why Be Aware of Cultural Differences?

Correctional professionals who are sensitive to cultural differences can appreciate a culture's distinctiveness and seek to make allowances for such factors when communicating with members of that cultural group. They can avoid imposing their own cultural attitudes and approaches on other groups.

Through cross-cultural experiences, correctional professionals become more broadminded and tolerant of cultural "peculiarities." When this is coupled with formal study of the concept of culture, new insights for improving human relations are gained and intercultural experiences are maximized.

Correctional professionals should be aware of the culture shock some inmates might experience. Culture shock is a psychological disorientation caused by misunderstanding or not understanding the cues from another culture. Many people experience culture shock when they find themselves in strange and unexpected situations. It arises from such things as lack of knowledge, limited prior experience, and personal rigidity.

For correctional professionals, cultural awareness represents a new body of knowledge or a tool to increase professional development and organizational effectiveness with other employees, inmates, and other people encountered in the course of daily business. Certainly, cultural awareness helps individuals understand that culture and behavior are relative and that they should be more tentative and less absolute in their human interactions.

# Reference

Harris, P. R., and R. T. Moran 1991. *Managing cultural differences.* Houston, Texas: Gulf Publishing Company.

# 2. Expression of African-American Culture in Correctional Settings

*By Portia Hunt, Ph.D.*

**A**frican-American culture needs to be examined in the context of historical, social, and political events that shape American culture. Ethnic identity factors that characterize African-American personalities are indeed complex but can be understood if one looks at the communications patterns, verbal and nonverbal, that occur within social interactions. In this chapter, African-American identity is defined as an ethnic group with distinguished language and cultural patterns. This will be followed by a discussion of African-American identity within the correctional setting.

The ethnic identity of a group is characterized by the following dimensions: shared behavior, common language, common political and social goals, similar interpretations of in-group and out-group interactions, and a shared notion of communal and personal identities.

## African-American Identity: What's in a Name?

African-American people appear to be changing the name of their racial group every few decades or so. What is the name change all about? What does it mean to keep one label for a period of time and then select a new one? What do these changes mean within the context of ethnic identity and pride? To observers outside the African-

*Portia Hunt, Ph.D., is a professor in Counseling Psychology at Temple University and the president of Eclipse Consultant Group, which is based in Philadelphia, Pa.*

American community, these name changes appear to be arbitrary, random, and trend-driven. But if one looks beyond the surface, it becomes clear that this is not the case. These changes represent a group's struggle for self-acceptance, self-determination, and most of all a strong rejection of negative stereotypes that were a part of white America's portrayal of blacks in the pre-Civil Rights era.

From slavery through the 1950s, African-American identity was determined by whites. The terms "Negro," "coloreds," "darkie," and others (many of which were derogatory) were racial labels whites gave to blacks to define for them their racial and ethnic identity. Used interchangeably, these terms have their roots in the anti-slave era. The labels were used to reinforce the notion that blacks were at the bottom of the socioeconomic class strata, and more important, not a part of American culture.

The labels "Negro" and "colored" were often posted on signs as a warning to both blacks and whites that public facilities and resources were to remain segregated. This social norm was to be maintained at all cost. If violated by blacks, it was often reinforced by individual and/or mob violence by whites or by legal reprimand.

This separate and unequal treatment had a great effect on the political, economic, and educational aspirations of blacks. Because blacks were systematically blocked from full participation in mainstream America, they developed a parallel economic and social class system to survive under institutionalized racism.

Racial labels whites bestowed on blacks were a part of the problem. The labels carried with them expectations of stereotypical behavior. Whites expected "colored" people to act inferior. The label "Negro" connotes that blacks should be beholden to whites for repealing slavery and granting them rights as American citizens.

The Civil Rights Movement of the late 1950s and 1960s and later the Black Power Movement of the '60s and '70s marked a major shift in rejection of white identity labels by blacks. The label "black" was chosen by blacks as a break from past racial designations and as a political/social statement of self-determination. In the past, the label "black" was associated with evil, darkness, inferiority, and primitivity. For the first time, American Negroes, as a group, rejected the terms "Negro" and "colored" as their racial/ethnic designation. This in part was a rejection of white dominance, and a clear statement by blacks to define themselves based on their own consciousness. Blacks in the '60s and '70s challenged past stereotypes about being labeled "black" and, more important, insisted that blackness was a source of pride, power, and honor. Labels such as "Afro-American" and "black" became catalysts for blacks to insist that they receive access to opportunities, education, employment, politics, and most of all, the same rights as other Americans.

For blacks to be called a "Black American" meant to accept one's racial identity. Race and ethnicity are intricately related, but they are not mutually inclusive. Race refers to one's physical characteristics, while ethnicity refers to national origin or cultural traditions. Because race and ethnicity have been used interchangeably to describe the descendants of African slaves, the term "black" was the first phase of racial acceptance by African Americans. Although the term was used to show racial solidarity among blacks, it was also a source of confusion because it does not acknowledge a black American's ethnicity. In the '70s and '80s social scientists and scholars attempted to reconcile this problem of race versus ethnicity by capitalizing the letter "b" in "black" in professional journals. This change was seen as an acknowledgment of the group's ethnic and racial identity. On the other hand, the term "white," as used in a racial designation, was presented with a lower case "w." This solution was often met with confusion and hostility by publishers and authors, many of whom were white. Publishers argued that racial labels "black" and "white" should both appear in lower case letters. Afrocentric authors, especially blacks, resented the publishers' editorial changes. This conflict was a microcosm of a greater issue that the ethnic identity of blacks was intertwined with race.

To add more fuel to the debate, larger numbers of black Caribbeans and other black Africans were immigrating to the United States. These new immigrants were black, but their ethnic identities were clearly reflective of their national origin. Black Americans began to clarify and embrace their ethnic heritage. Because most blacks did not know their specific country of origin in West Africa, the label African American emerged. This change reflects a merging of two ethnic identities: African and American. The Reverend Jesse Jackson has been credited with the label change and the widespread popularity of the term.

# Core Symbols of African-American Culture—Ethnic Markers

Core symbols identified in research on African-American culture are strongly interrelated. Collectivism, individuality, positivism, emotional spontaneity, genuineness, assertiveness, orientation to time, and skepticism, secrecy, and distrust (White & Parham 1990) are a few of the core symbols that describe African-American ethnic group characteristics.

## *Collectivism*

Collectivism is the same as sharing one's attitudes, beliefs, feelings, and resources that characterizes the dialogue between in-group members (Hecht et al. 1993). When African Americans talk to each other, the conversation is often intense, active, and ritualistic.

In group meetings with a speaker presenting, a call-and-response pattern is used between the speaker and audience to reinforce how culture is shared. In call-and-response interactions, there is spontaneous group response to any part of the speaker's message. Audience members yell out approval if they agree with the message. In turn, the speaker may acknowledge the audience's feedback. This response pattern is very much a part of black church rituals. Statements like "Amen," "I hear," "Preach on," "Tell the truth," etc., may be shouted from the audience while the minister is encouraged to reach the heights of emotional expression in the sermon.

Humor, wit, and intellectual jousting are part of the collectivism value among African Americans. These attributes can be observed when group members boast, tease, "play the dozens," and "woof" with each other (Kochman 1981). These behaviors are ethnic markers that are part of the collectivism value and are reinforced by group participation. When displayed, they are expected to be reciprocated by others as an indication of belonging to the group.

Boasting is a form of self-aggrandizement and exaggeration. Related to teasing others, it is used to stimulate others to compete and interact. Unlike bragging, which is flaunting one's possessions, the person is showing off his or her wit and challenging the other person to do the same. Playing the dozens and woofing are dueling styles African Americans use in groups to exchange insults and prevent physical fights. Playing the dozens is a spontaneous way of creating rhymes to embarrass one's opponent without resorting to physical blows. Woofing, a shorter version of the dozens, is the exchange of verbal insults and challenges to fight. The person tries to exaggerate his or her personal powers while demeaning his or her opponent's. It's a form of one-upmanship that's presented with humor. When this stylistic posturing occurs in a group, observers laugh at the two challengers and encourage them to outdo each other. Eventually, the group functions to release tension before the group disperses, promoting group harmony.

## Individuality

Individuality is the unique expression of a person's personality attributes. It can be observed through dress, walking a certain way, dancing, hand slapping, unusual facial expressions, or by specialized verbal expressions. The individual's stylistic way of behaving is his or her signature to being uniquely himself or herself. In music, dance, and poetry, improvisation is respected and encouraged. The goal is to show one's best to the outside world. African-American children are socialized to show off their unique qualities, while always being mindful of the group as a collective.

## Positivism

Positivism is expressed as a way to overcome crises and stress. "Negro spirituals" are examples of this value. Despite many slaves enduring a hell on earth, the notion of going to heaven and of being able to overcome one's trials and tribulations is an example of being positive despite one's hardships. Positivism is closely related to African-American belief in spiritualism and religion. Individual expression of one's convictions can occur in groups through shouting, crying, laughing, and praying aloud. Sometimes positive expression can become a form of denying one's problems.

## Genuineness

Genuineness is often demonstrated in situations that call for African Americans to reveal their true feelings about a situation, even when exposure could lead to disapproval by those in authority. It means to be real—not put on airs and "act black." For some, this means to choose authenticity over "being phony," a behavior often associated with "acting white" or using standard English and "uppity" words just to impress others. African Americans refer to those who exhibit realness as "down to earth," "regular," and "telling it like it is." This value is often expressed in group conversations among African Americans about other African Americans who were observed in conversations with whites.

## Assertiveness

Assertiveness is standing up for one's beliefs and opinions in the face of adversity. This may be expressed by opposing others in authority or by verbally rejecting another's viewpoint. Assertiveness may be expressed if the person is challenged in front of others. It may mean making controversial statements that may be viewed as aggressive by others. For example, rap groups have been attacked by adults and others for being too explicit in their songs.

This value has always been a core symbol in African-American culture. It is one in which whites and those in authority have reacted to strongly. Among whites, African-American assertiveness is often linked with aggression, especially when it is expressed in the context of woofing.

## Orientation to Time

Orientation to time is an important value that African Americans interpret differently than whites. When appointments are made, African Americans may arrive on time, slightly late, or very late depending on the activity. It is acceptable to arrive one to two hours late for a party. This is especially characteristic of African Americans who are not used to operating in white settings. African Americans tend to be "in time," rather than "on time." The reverse tends to be true for whites. To arrive late is considered rude in white norms. The African American norm of being "in time" may be a carry over of African culture and agrarian life. People in third world countries tend to view time differently than those in industrialized countries. The former does not seek to control time, so it is viewed in a relaxed way. Being late for an appointment is no big deal. For whites, being late is viewed as disrespectful and disinterested. For African Americans, ''in time'' or being late is viewed as slightly annoying but acceptable behavior.

### Skepticism, Secrecy, and Distrust

Skepticism, secrecy, and distrust of outsiders is another group of core symbols among African Americans. The symbols or values may be expressed in indirect ways. With outsiders, the initial social posture is to be friendly and polite. If the outsider is selling something or wants an African American's cooperation that involves the release of personal information, distrust and skepticism is most often the immediate response. African Americans tend to be suspicious of strangers. A black Philadelphia police officer made the observation that it was easier to bust Latino drug dealers because they sell on the streets. Blacks usually sell in houses or bars: they try to screen buyers before selling them drugs. These values are believed to have been developed from slavery. Black slaves had to be cautious and secretive because to be otherwise often meant death or punishment to fellow slaves.

# Ethnic Identity in Correctional Settings

The need of black inmates to coalesce around ethnic identity intensifies in correctional settings. On the surface inmates are faced with several dilemmas that must be resolved if they are to survive prison life:

1. They must come to grips with the loss of the personal freedom they enjoyed before incarceration.

2. They must learn to accept the stigma and shame associated with being labeled an inmate.

3. They must learn to cope with boredom, unstructured time, and being strictly supervised by correctional officers.

4. They must struggle to acquire a solid identity to help them survive the stresses of prison life.

Most new inmates (regardless of race or ethnicity) experience intense loss of personal identity and probably shame associated with the new identity of an inmate. In prison, an inmate is a number in a cell. One of the most pressing stressors for new inmates is loss of identity, social status, and freedom. Given these losses, the inmate must struggle to define who he or she is in this new setting. And probably for the first time in the inmate's life, this struggle for self-definition cannot be resolved by using typical coping strategies of denial and avoidance. The inmate cannot run away. If the inmate tries to avoid this issue, other inmates will pressure him or her to identify with some group. Black inmates who use withdrawal and depression to avoid the identity struggle leave themselves open for verbal and possibly physical attacks from other blacks. Their avoidance will be judged as a weakness—and weak inmates do not survive in prison.

While in prison, inmates must learn to work through the stigma associated with being incarcerated. Prisons are containment stalls for a wide range of societal problems. People from all walks of life are in prisons. The shame associated with being in prison results in depression for some inmates. Others use domination, rage, and violence to cope with being incarcerated. Still others may adjust by becoming the "model inmate"; this may include conforming to prison rules, educating oneself, obtaining religious guidance, or immersing self in one's ethnic heritage.

For African-American inmates, religiosity, self-education, and ethnic identification serve to minimize and relinquish shame associated with being in prison. These three ways of coping form the cornerstone of the African-American community, and they speak to the formative years in the lives of many blacks.

One of the paradoxes of prison life is the absence of personal structure in a highly structured institution. There are virtually no demands placed on the individual for intellectual, social, or emotional development. On the other hand, the institution strictly controls what one wears and activities such as eating, sleeping, taking showers, exercising, and working. If mental and emotional stimulation happen at all, the inmate must make them happen. For blacks, studying about one's racial and ethnic background is one way of understanding how African Americans can challenge themselves to grow intellectually and accept responsibility for their contributions to their personal problems within a racial context.

How does the correctional officer relate to African-American inmates? If the officer is white, it is important to observe the boundaries and understand why they are there. Ethnic identity and group affiliation may be the only line between survival and being physically brutalized by other inmates. The white officer should not try to belong to the group by "acting black" or using nonstandard English. African-American inmates can detect someone who is trying too hard to be one of the group.

It is important that white correctional officers not put the inmate in a position where he or she has to violate loyalty to their ethnic group in front of other African Americans. This could result in the inmate being a victim of physical retaliation or being ostracized. African-American inmates are able to go against group norms once their social position in the group has been solidified and trust has been established with other African-American inmates.

The African-American correctional officer will be evaluated differently by African-American inmates. The African-American officer is assumed to be familiar with the culture and will be tested by inmates. Correctional officers who are fair but firm will receive respect. Black correctional officers must prove that they have not "sold out" to the system. Selling out means acting white, being unfair to African-American inmates; taking sides with whites against blacks, especially when it's clear that the whites are in the wrong; and not being assertive in situations where one's integrity is being questioned.

Survival in poor urban cities is tough. African-American youth and young adults must maneuver their way through gangs, drug and alcohol temptation, inadequate schools, poverty, and multiple family problems. Growing up black and poor in America is a major task in and of itself, but in prison, survival is much more difficult. Learning to survive is heavily influenced by the hardened criminal element. Those who escape choose religiosity (e.g., the Black Muslims), insanity, brute force, or they learn to protect themselves by aligning with other small groups of inmates.

Social problems related to poverty and organized crime activity found in poor urban communities are replicated and intensified in prison culture. Prison takes the place of the African-American community. Cultural attitudes, behavior, and values of African Americans get played out in prison along with the pathological norms of street life. The consequences are potentially dangerous for those who do not know how to survive in the streets.

For blacks, survival in prison can be a life-altering experience. Prisons are disproportionately populated with black males. Inside prison walls, social status, survival, and obtaining respect are intricately linked. Not knowing who you are as an African American could mean that you leave yourself open to be a victim of violence. Knowing who you are and having a support network may determine if you are left alone to develop on your own with minimum demands from your group. One major aspect of survival is letting others outside your referent group know who you are and how you identify yourself. For blacks, the constructive survival identities are religious, ethnic, or athletic.

In conclusion, correctional officers play an important role in the adjustment of African American inmates. If they lack knowledge about the group characteristics of any group they may misinterpret behavior based on white cultural norms. If emotional expressiveness is understood and respected within a cultural context, the CO will be able to accurately discriminate nonviolent posturing from intent to act. They will understand when to intervene in conflictual situations and when to ignore it. They will be able to integrate their understanding of institutional culture with the demands inmates place on each other within their cultural group.

# References

Hecht, M. L., M. J. Collier, and S. A. Ribeau 1993. *African-American communication*. Newbury Park, Calif.: Sage Publications.

Kochman, T. 1981. *Black and white styles in conflict*. Chicago: University of Chicago Press.

White, J. L., and T. A. Parham. 1990. *The psychology of blacks: An African-American perspective*. Englewood Cliffs, N.J.: Prentice-Hall.

# 3. The African-American Woman

*By Joyce Jackson*

## Black Is

*Black is a color*
*The color of my hair.*
*Black is my mother*
*Who will love me and care*

*Black is my father*
*Who I love and respect*
*And never look back.*

*Black is the darkness*
*That I sleep in each night.*
*Black is my race*
*That I see in the light.*

*Black are my people*
*My roots, my family tree.*
*I wouldn't be me.*

*—Jeannette Wooden*

Who is this African-American woman? Where did she come from? What does she represent? These are just a few of the questions surrounding the mystique of the African-American woman—a woman who is often misrepresented and unrecognized.

*Joyce Jackson is the public relations officer for the Oklahoma Department of Corrections and president of the Professional Association of Correctional Communicators.*

The fact is that the African-American woman is a phenomenon. She is a survivor, a force to be reckoned with as the result of her past experiences.

> . . . the American Negro woman is the most interesting woman in this country. . . . She is the only woman in America, who is almost unknown, the only woman for whom nothing is done, the only woman without sufficient defenders when assailed; the only woman who is still outside of that world of chivalry that in all the ages has apothesized womankind (Hines 1990).

The African-American woman's self-image, her confidence, as well as her perceptions of the world have all evolved out of personal experiences. Many of these experiences are rooted in myths and stereotypes surrounding her ethnic and cultural heritage and gender.

# The History of the African-American Woman

The story of the African-American woman started some 400 years ago with the slave trade, when several women captured in Africa were driven to the sea and transported to the New World. They were and had to be women of incredible strength and vitality.

According to history, the first African-American women arrived when the first twenty African Americans were delivered to Jamestown, Virginia, in 1619. By 1625, the first detailed census indicated there were twenty-three African Americans in Virginia: eleven men, ten women, and two children. This group made up 2 percent of the total population.

Contrary to popular belief, these African Americans were not slaves—slavery did not exist in Virginia at that time. These African Americans, like the whites, were considered indentured servants.

This also means that the first African-American women in this country had roughly the same social status as the first white women in this country. Therefore the first African-American women completed their term of servitude and were later freed.

The Jamestown experience was by no means unique. Similar situations were unfolding in other colonies. Throughout this period and on into the eighteenth century, these women remained a very small portion of the total African-American population in most of these colonies. However, in some colonies, the numbers were larger because of special cargoes of African-American women imported for the male population.

By the eighteenth century, there were a number of free African-American women in almost every colony. This situation didn't last long because colonial leaders soon abandoned the system of white indentured servitude and created a new system based on the perpetual slavery of African-American men and women. It took a while to work out the details, but the new slave system passed laws that redefined the status of African-American women and the issue of their reproductive organs. In 1662, Virginia declared "that all children born in this country shall be held, bond or free only according to the condition of the mother" (Giddings 1984).

With the creation of the slave system and a period where it was believed that women should be seen and not heard, the first social movement in these times was started by men. But this movement was strongly supported by women like Catherine Ferguson, the founder of the first modern Sunday school in New York City and a pioneer in social work, and Charlotte Forten, the daughter of a wealthy African-American sail manufacturer, who essayed the dual role of homemaker and community activist.

The best-known African-American women of that time were Lucy Terry Prince and Phillis Wheatley. Prince was the wife of a well-to-do landowner and one of the founders of Sunderland, Vermont. She wrote a poem in 1746 commemorating an Indian raid and became the first black American poet.

Phyllis Wheatley mastered the English language sixteen months after arriving in Boston on a slave ship. In 1773, she published a book of poetry, which was the first book by an American black and the second book by an American woman.

In the eighteenth century African-American women were often in the forefront as workers and providers, but as economic racism fell, these women generally found employment as washwomen and maids. In fact, they were concentrated in service jobs at the bottom of the scale.

A few free African-American women managed to break sexual and racial barriers to enter the field of higher education. In 1858 the first institution of higher learning for African-American women was organized in Washington, D.C., by Myrtilla Miner. In 1862, Mary Jane Pattersen received a degree from Oberlin College and became the first African-American woman to graduate from a school of higher education.

In the South, the African-American woman was engaged in a slavery system that threatened her in a peculiarly devastating manner. Unlike the male slave, the female slave was exploited socially, economically, and sexually, which is why historians often say the African-American woman was under a triple oppression.

From the beginning of the slave trade, the exploitation of the African-American woman became a permanent feature in the American social and economic arena. She was assaulted simultaneously as a worker, a black, and a woman. She was worked from sunup to sundown, hoeing, chopping, digging ditches, and clearing fields. When the sun went down, she was expected to tend to the needs of her man and her children. At the same time, she was often exposed to the demands and threats of slave owners and overseers. African-American men and white women had more power (and say in the disposal of their physical resources) than black women. Rape was a real and ever-present possibility for the African-American woman during slavery.

The African-American slave was considered chattel: a thing, a privately owned commodity. Some slave masters tolerated slaves on their own farms or on their neighbor's property to marry each other. But even the most "humane" master, when confronted with economic declines, would disrupt African-American families by selling off a spouse or several children. It was not always good business to keep families together. African-American women were sold separately to bring a more competitive price on the open market.

Children over the age of fourteen were viewed as prime field hands and were routinely taken from their mothers and fathers. In fact, the public sale of young black girls above the age of twelve was usually to satisfy the sexual needs of slave masters.

One of the most flagrant forms of oppression for African-American women during these times was slave breeding. According to one historian, "slaves were usually reared with an eye to their marketability...and many masters counted the fertility level of their African-American women slaves as an economic asset. In the context of American slavery, the African-American woman was often reduced to the lowest level of a biological being" (Marable 1983).

Many African-American women fought against being used as sexual objects and many sacrificed their lives to retain their humanity. Many more carried the scars of rape, both physically and psychologically, with them for the rest of their lives.

Many of these women ran away from their plantations or farms in search of freedom. Because of the qualities slave women had to have to survive, some of these women soon became the leaders and shapers of the slave community. They led slave revolts and pressed for vindication and justice in America. A great many of these women escaped through the Underground Railroad. It has been estimated that at least one out of every four fugitives was female. Harriet Tubman is said to have escaped from slavery in Maryland and returned nineteen times to lead more than 300 slaves to freedom.

During that same period, other African-American women assumed active and nontraditional roles in the Abolitionist Movement. One of the first to break the taboo against female public speakers was Maria W. Stewart, a free African-American woman who lectured in New England in the 1830s. The most renowned abolitionist was Sojourner Truth, a former New York slave.

The pioneer leaders of the African-American women who pushed for liberation jointly supported the white women's liberation movement. However, there was always a certain tension between the two groups because white suffragettes often confused the African-American struggle for basic human rights through the abolishment of slavery with the majority women's struggle for an extension of human rights.

During the Civil War, tens of thousands of African-American women, along with Sojourner Truth and Harriet Tubman, crossed rebel lines and served the Union Army as washwomen, cooks, laborers, and nurses. At the same time, African-American women in the North raised money for war relief and sent clothing and food to the refugees in the South. Among the leading women in this effort were Mary E. Perke, who founded the first school for free men in the south; Charlotte L. Forten, who taught freedom on the Sea Islands; and Sojourner Truth, who nursed soldiers in the Washington, D.C., area. The most notable contribution was made by Harriet

Tubman, who became the first and last American woman to lead American soldiers in battle.

During the Reconstruction Period, African-American men were exposed to the fringes of power for the first time in their lives, and African-American women had their first opportunity to explore their femininity. The first response to this was an almost unprecedented attempt to legalize family relations. During this time, men and women traveled thousands of miles to find long-lost mates and locate daughters and sons who had been relocated across the country. There was also a mass movement to marry.

Another response to the times was the adoption of new dress codes, which allowed former female slaves to purchase jewelry and silks once forbidden to African-American women by law.

The most threatening response was the mass withdrawal of African-American women from the fields. It was considered dishonorable in this period for an African-American man to let his woman and children participate in this type of labor. According to historians, "plantation owners were shocked when large numbers of these women had the nerve to refuse to work in the fields." Since most of these women were denied the right to work in any other jobs outside the home, the public soon fully expected them to either be domestic workers or take on the traditional role of mothers by giving birth to as many children as was physically possible (Hines 1990).

Although the Victorian Era was inhospitable to the intelligent and politically active female, a number of African-American women succeeded in overcoming the institutional barriers of patriarchy. It was at this time that Frances Ellen Watkins Harper established herself as the nineteenth century's most popular African-American poet and activist. In 1854 she worked for the Maine Anti-Slavery Society and later for the Pennsylvania Anti-Slavery Society. She authored several books of poetry and wrote articles for the press. Until her death in 1911, Harper was a noted advocate of women's suffrage, equal rights, and freedom.

Another notable activist was Isabella Baumfree. Baumfree was an outstanding orator of the African-American struggle, even though she was illiterate. She was born a slave and later freed, but forced to escape after her master refused to let her go. Her experiences as a slave inspired her antislavery crusade. She later changed her name and became known as Sojourner Truth. Sojourner Truth was equally zealous in her fight for women's rights.

Most of the jobs available to African-American women after the abolishment of slavery consisted of working in the kitchens and homes of their white counterparts. But even from the kitchen, African-American women were sensitive to the needs of their families and pushed for their husbands, fathers, and brothers to vote the Republican ticket. African-American women by law and custom were barred from voting, but they strongly believed that voting for the Radical Republican regime was the only way they could secure homes, educational advantages for their children, and receive the protection and all the rights accorded to them by the Constitution.

When the Republican party was overthrown by the Ku Klux Klan and other white terrorist groups, African-American men and women were forced back into the fields, and a reign of terror was instituted to keep them in their place. It was also a time when terrorists used African-American women as targets to humiliate their men.

Throughout this period and on into the twentieth century, African-American men and women were being lynched in record numbers. Between 1918 and 1927, 91.6 percent of the people lynched in the United States were African Americans. Eleven were women, three of whom were pregnant. Many of the men were not only lynched, they were castrated as well. In the 1920s, lynchings became such a popular cultural event that hundreds of white women and children were invited to take part in the festivities.

Two of the most progressive female activists during the post-Reconstruction Period were Ida B. Wells-Barnett and Mary Church Terrell, both of whom were cofounders of the National Association for the Advancement of Colored People. Wells-Barnett, a civil rights leader, an antilynching crusader, and a woman of strong conviction, acquired the reputation as the most militant journalist in the South. After purchasing a partial ownership in a Memphis newspaper, Wells-Barnett launched a ten-year crusade against lynching that caused her to be run out of the South and later out of the country. Noted for her crusade and her concern about lynchings, she organized the Alpha Suffrage Club in Chicago, after Illinois granted women the right to vote in local elections. This club is the first organization for African-American women in the nation.

Terrell, a teacher and civil rights leader, was elected first president of the historic National Association of Colored Women in 1896. She was also an active member of the National American Woman Suffrage Association and an important figure in the international women's movement. In her later years, Terrell became politically conservative; however, she continued to fight racial discrimination and Jim Crow laws until her death.

One of the other women who made major strides during this time was Mary McLeod Bethune, a civil rights leader, a prominent educator, and a pioneer in the cause for black women's education. In 1904, Bethune started the Daytona Normal and Industrial School on a dump heap, with faith and a $5 down payment on a $250 note, which she and her students worked to pay off. This school was later renamed the Bethune-Cookman College. She also founded the National Council of Negro Women.

As a result of the disastrous effects of the lynchings and Jim Crow laws, the African-American community began to withdraw and turn inward for support—a change that unconsciously created a wave of economic growth that would never have been thought possible.

It was a time when female pathfinders like Maggie Lena Walker, who became the first African-American woman to organize and head a bank, and Madame C. J. Walker (no relation), who created a business empire and became the first African-American to be certified a millionaire, emerged. At the same time, another group of African-American women was busy nurturing the black church, which is the one institution that is and has been considered the backbone of the African-American community.

African-American women continued to move into the twentieth century with achievements too numerous to detail here. But it was obvious that change had indeed been made.

Bell Hooks (1981) points out that labeling African-American women as matriarchs is similar to labeling female children who play house and act out the role of mothers. Julius A. Boyd, writer and historian, says "the mythological portrait of the African-American matriarch is a folk character fashioned by whites from their distorted image about the involuntary social and economic conditions of African-American women in a system that devalues women of color" (Cade 1970).

24

The idea of categorizing African-American women is not easy because they tend to be individuals. Joyce Ladner (1971) points out that there is no monolithic concept of the African-American woman, but there are many models of African-American womanhood.

African-American women are distinct individuals who make choices as to the many ways in which they gain their strength. There are African-American women who may not always look to their ethnic and cultural traditions for subsistence but are very likely to seek the comfort that only their community or family can provide.

To survive, many African-American women have become masters in the art of being bicultural. Audre Lourde (Cade 1970) points out, "those of us for whom oppression is as American as apple pie have always had to be watchers, to become familiar with the language and manners of the oppressor, even sometimes adopting them for some illusion of protection." The African-American woman discovered that learning to comply publicly with white standards has not been as much a choice as a dictate necessary for survival. Julius Boyd says, "The continued challenge of being caught in a system that values only one set of standards is a constant burden for women of color. And for the woman of color to openly fight back is an invitation to become a target of institutionalized racism designed in the form of rules and regulations to keep one in their proper place" (Cade 1970).

## Female African-American Offenders

The number of women incarcerated over the past few years has almost doubled. In fact, statistics indicate that African-American women are likely to be sentenced more severely than white women for similar crimes. According to the National Institute of Justice, African-American women represent 43 percent of all the female inmates in federal prisons. In 1990, the National Institute of Justice reported 19,131 African-American women were incarcerated in state prisons and 2,051 in federal prisons. The larger numbers of incarcerated African-American women are typically found in the South, where those numbers are doubled in comparison to the Northeast, Midwest, and West.

The reasons African-American women are sentenced to prison are as varied as the color of their skin, but there are some physical, mental, and social problems that stand out. Most African-American women in custody have experienced or been the victim of drug or alcohol dependency, unemployment, illiteracy, homelessness, and isolation. Most suffer from defeat, poor self-esteem, and a total lack of purpose in life. There is also an extremely high rate of sexually transmitted diseases among incarcerated African-American women as a result of swapping sex for drugs. These women in most cases, personify the elements of a victim.

Like her white counterpart, the African-American female offender is extremely dependent, even though her persona indicates that she is a strong-willed, free-thinking, independent being. She in fact, has generally very little or no support from a man or from a job. The reason is African-American female offenders are usually poorly educated and marginally employable. They embody the disadvantages of most women plus some.

National statistics indicate that the profile of the average adult female offender not only fits the African-American woman in prison, but is in fact this woman. According to the profile, this woman is a racial minority between the ages of 25 and 29 who has either never been married or who, before incarceration, was a single parent living alone with one to three children. They usually come from a single parent or a broken home, with 50 percent having other family members incarcerated, 54 percent of which are brothers and sisters. She has run away from home at least one to three times. She is easily influenced by her peers and uses drugs to make herself feel emotionally better. The African-American female offender has most likely been a victim of sexual abuse by a male member of her immediate family. She is usually into drugs and/or alcohol between the ages of thirteen and fourteen (ACA 1990).

By the time she ends up in prison, the African-American woman has been arrested for multiple offenses and has been on and off of probation several times. She is typically sentenced to prison for economically related or property crimes. The primary reasons for her to commit a crime stem from drugs, economic pressures, or following someone else's agenda. She, like the average female offender, is a high school dropout, stemming in most cases from a pregnancy.

Once in prison, the African-American female offender states that all too often she is assigned to menial jobs, which in most cases do not provide them with any job training experiences—jobs that appear to be the stereotypical occupations for African-American women, like cooking and maintenance.

Basically, the African-American female offender is no different than any other female, in or out of prison, except for the fact that her attitude, behavior, and responses may differ as the result of her culture and experiences. Compounded by racism and sexism, the African-American female offender routinely manages to handle these difficulties as she copes with the perils of day-to-day living.

# References

American Correctional Association. 1990. *The female offender: What does the future hold?* Laurel, Md.: ACA.

Cade, T., ed. 1970. *The black woman, an anthology*. New York: New American Library.

Giddings, P. 1984. *When and where I enter—The impact of black women on race and sex in America*. New York: William Morrow and Company.

Hines, D. C., ed. 1990. *Black women in United States history*. Vol. 2. Brooklyn: Carlson Publishing.

Hooks, B. 1981. *Ain't I a woman*. Boston: South End Press.

Ladner, J. 1971. *Tomorrow's tomorrow: The black woman*. Garden City, N.Y.: Doubleday.

Marable, M. 1983. *How capitalism undeveloped black America: Problems in race, political economy and society*. Boston: South End Press.

# 4. Caribbean Islanders

*By Karen B. Shepard*

This chapter will provide the reader with a brief overview of the cultural history of the Caribbean and discuss the many influences that have contributed to the culture and the people of the Caribbean.

## Geography

In the United States, many view the Caribbean as a place for vacation, rum, sun, beach, and even hedonism. As inviting as this description might be, it is superficial. The Caribbean is a chain of islands located in the Caribbean Sea, stretching from south of the Florida panhandle in a clockwise arc to the coast of Venezuela. The islands of the Caribbean, or what is culturally termed the West Indies, range in size from the tiny land mass of Anguilla of 88 square kilometers to larger islands like Cuba, which measures 114,500 square kilometers.

## The Early Inhabitants

The Arawak Indians were the original inhabitants of the Caribbean islands. They are now extinct among the population of islanders except for a minority group of descendants who live in the hinterland of Guyana on the South American mainland.

Except for the limited information that can be retrieved from the study of artifacts, bones, vessels, cave etchings, tools, and eating utensils, there is no precise and identifiable lifestyle that one can reasonably associate with the lifestyle of today's Caribbean islander.

The demise of these early inhabitants took a dramatic turn in the

*Karen B. Shepard is Project Director of the Cultural Differences Project at the American Correctional Association.*

fifteenth century after the voyages of Christopher Columbus, who in his search for a new route to India came across the Caribbean islands. Columbus's observation and his report to the Spanish monarchy created much interest in Europe, and the Spanish, British, French, Dutch, and Germans soon came to the Caribbean to settle and take advantage of the riches that this region had to offer. The Arawak Indians were enslaved and badly treated by European colonists. They soon died.

During the nineteenth century, the Chinese came to the islands in search of economic prosperity and a haven for their mercantile trade. They settled in Jamaica in great numbers. Soon other migrant groups, such as the Syrians, Arabs, and Jews, found their grounding in the Caribbean Islands, and a unique cultural blend emerged.

# Cultural Development of the Caribbean

The Caribbean can best be defined as a composite of the cultures of many lands whose inhabitants had direct or indirect influence on the lifestyles of the Caribbean people. If culture implies that there is an established mode of behavior, then one could say that the British had a significant effect on the culture of the region. This includes language, dress, social habits, sports and games, music, religion, and general education.

When the Arawak Indians died, the African slave trade and indentured East Indian labor emerged as sources of exploitable labor. The influx of West Africans (as slaves) at the same time the British came to the islands saw a simultaneous introduction of two distinct cultures. English music, dance, crafts, and cookery were established alongside that of West Africa. The culture of the numerically superior Africans competed with the culture of the English for supremacy, and by the middle of the nineteenth century, the two cultures had merged in many ways to form a new independent culture of the West Indies.

Around the middle of the nineteenth century, Asiatic influences arrived with the East Indians and Chinese. Their influences centered mostly in the areas of the culinary arts, traditional dances and songs, religion, sugar plantation work ethic, and local trade.

The Germans made a significant impact on the Caribbean culture through Moravian religion, education, and trade. The French also contributed to the emergence of a Caribbean culture. The French territories of Martinique and Guadeloupe have infused strong French traditions in the culture of the Caribbean through language and lifestyle. The Dutch have also influenced Caribbean culture, particularly in the islands of Aruba, Bonaire, and Curacao.

# U. S. Influence on the Caribbean

Small, poor, and developing countries often accept the assistance of rich and powerful countries, primarily for economic survival. This economic dependence also assists in the transmission of culture. Simply put, economic dependence can lead to cultural dependence through reinforcement from imported mass media, films, visitors, and informal education. British imperialism, and for that matter European imperialism, excluded other cultural influences on the Caribbean region up until the 1930s. It was about this time that the United States began to affect Caribbean culture through political and economic influence. Political penetration ran on parallel lines with economic and cultural influences. Political influence took the form of governmental policy agreements. The economic infusion took the form of government aid, public and private investment, and preferential trade status.

Cultural influence from the U.S. came through migration, tourism, trade, the cinema, radio, television, and telecommunication devices, such as telephones, citizens band radio, and the satellite dish. For example, an analysis of television programming in Jamaica, Antigua, Barbados and Trinidad, and Tobago undertaken in 1972 revealed that 88 percent of prime-time programs shown in these areas were imported from the United States (Jamaica Information Service 1973). Emigrants to the United States who have maintained contact with their relatives and friends in the Caribbean or returned home have contributed to a familiarity with the American way of life, customs, cultural traits, food, and material goods.

The increasing penetration of the United States into the Caribbean, particularly the English-speaking Caribbean, is strong through industries, such as oil and bauxite and tourism. These industries have made the region more economically dependent on the United

States and created a shift to North American styles in cars, food, and clothing.

The consumer culture of the Caribbean has been fully Americanized. Statistics show that 62 percent of the Jamaican population wish to emigrate to the United States (Jamaica Information Service 1973). Many feel that this move will ensure economic prosperity and allow them to indulge in the promise of the American Dream.

# Multiculturalism in the Caribbean

The historical circumstances of colonial rule, slavery, and indentured labor have given rise to the cultural integration of various cultural groups in the Caribbean. Caribbean islanders are represented by many racial and ethnic groups. These groups include people of European descent, African descent, Chinese, Lebanese, Syrians, and East Indians. Intermarriage among these groups is common and widely accepted. The Caribbean culture is the result of a mix of certain characteristics from each of the different groups that came to call this region home. Many of the commonly recognized characteristics of this Caribbean culture can be described through their customs and lifestyle.

The people of the Caribbean (West Indians) have great respect for friends and the extended family. They typically maintain a strong sense of community and family kinship. This often transcends racial and ethnic lines. They are very proud of their heritage and nationality.

West Indians commonly maintain very little physical space when communicating. Hugging, kissing, handshakes, or some other form of physical contact are common nonverbal means of communicating, even with strangers. Verbal communication tends to be very animated. The tendency for most West Indians is to be cooperative and helpful. They will play down their inadequacies and try to put their best effort forward.

For the majority of Caribbean people, English is the official language of communication. Spanish, French, and Dutch are spoken in a few islands. French and a French dialect ("creole") are spoken in Haiti, Gaudeloupe, and Martinique. Spanish is spoken in the Dominican Republic, Cuba, and Puerto Rico. Spanish is also spoken with several local dialects. For example, in the Dominican Republic, "Sibaeno" and "Capitaleno" are two such dialects that are spoken. Dutch is primarily spoken in Aruba, Bonaire, and Curacao.

Local dialects are spoken by many, but are more often used by the less educated. Local dialects have their roots from the languages of Africa (brought to the Caribbean through the slave trade) and have been influenced by English, French, and Spanish. Dialects are an important part of Caribbean culture and life; they are a means of passing on tradition from generation to generation. Many of these dialects are spoken, not written. For example, Jamaican folklorist Louise Bennett has tried unsuccessfully to establish the Jamaican dialect of "patois" as a recognizable language and a legitimate form of communication at all levels of society.

West Indians have a passion for socializing and celebrating, as is evident in the many festivals and carnivals that take place throughout the Caribbean. Folk songs, dance, music (reggae and calypso), poetry, and other art forms depict the creative and colorful nature of the West Indian. These art forms represent the legacy and successful mix of African and European influences.

Religion is represented by both Christian and Protestant faiths including Catholic, Anglican, Methodist, and Baptist. Beliefs in superstitions and "black magic" exist in some areas. The most popular of these beliefs are "Obeah" in Jamaica and "Voodoo" in Haiti. These belief systems are most frequently practiced by individuals of lower socioeconomic status and lower education levels and are not accepted by the general populace.

The educational system throughout most of the English-speaking Caribbean is patterned from the British system of education. The system includes elementary, secondary, and post-secondary levels. For the most part, the educational system is free to all, with the exception of some private and religious academies or "prep schools." Religion and education often go hand-in-hand in the Caribbean. This mix is seen by many as one of the most effective ways of instilling values and morals in the young.

The diet of most West Indians consists of heavy, highly seasoned foods. Some of the staples include fish, chicken, meat, yams, rice, beans, and indigenous fruits and vegetables. Meals in any Caribbean household are an event where family and friends gather to socialize and enjoy each other's company.

32

# The Subculture of Rastafarianism

The elements of any culture include the emergence and existence of subcultures. These subcultures are not simply an extension of the mainstream culture, but can be a separate sector that is disenchanted, and disconnected, from the mainstream culture. Religious sects breaking away from the central group is a good example of this. When the Methodist Church broke away from the Anglican body, it remained in the Christian tradition but dispensed with certain practices that they found irrelevant to their needs.

A subculture may also emerge to preserve some ethnic traditions. Many people of East Indian origin in Jamaica and Trinidad abide by mainstream laws governing marriage, such as the legal registration and declaration of the marriage. They also perform certain ethnic rituals after the official marriage ceremony. This makes the wedding ceremony different from the traditional practice.

The Rastafarian culture, which began in Jamaica, is an example of the emergence of a subculture. The Rastafarian subculture is singled out for special mention because it is dynamic and controversial. Rastafarians have tried to establish themselves not only as a religion, but also as a lifestyle. It has affected the social fabric of many Caribbean islands and countries throughout the world. This effect has come primarily through the exportation of reggae music, which is authentically Rastafarian. Rastafarians have remained independent of involvement with any institution they regard as part of the general establishment (e.g., government and educational systems). This stance has posed a dilemma for the mass of Rastafarians who have been charged by the Ethiopian Orthodox Church to follow the examples set by Jesus Christ.

The Rastafarians took their name from Ras Tafari Makonnen, who was the governor of the Province of Harrare in his teen years and later became Prince Regent of the Ethiopian government in Addis Ababa. He was crowned Emperor Haile Salassie I in 1930. He was regarded as the emperor, the returned Christ, and the King of Kings as described in the Revelation of St. John the Divine. Salassie was anointed defender of the Christian faith at his coronation.

The Rastafarians formed a new religious community centered around the supposed divinity of the Emperor. Salassie refuted these claims on several occasions; he did not wish to be seen as a god by the Rastafarians. Despite several historical events that contradicted their beliefs, the Rastafarians continued to cling to the idea that Selassie was their divine leader. In addition, the Rastafarians began to follow the Nazarite vow that embraced the priestly cast of Israel that disallowed the cutting of their hair and beard. They believed that this practice was an imitation of Selassie and his subjects, who lived very primitive lifestyles. Rastafarianism is not a "black religion" as they would like the world to believe. It is an offshoot of white Christianity.

The smoking of "ganja" (marijuana) by Rastafarians began among agriculture workers who were introduced to it by indentured workers from India. The adoption of this practice by the Rastafarians introduced a new and dramatic turn in this group's social isolation. They justified this practice by labelling it a religious ritual having connections to ancient beliefs.

During their sixty years of existence, the Rastafarian cult has tried to secure recognition in Caribbean society as a separate religion. They have not been successful in this area. One of the reasons for their failure is that, unlike the Moslems, Hindus, and several other recognized religions, they have not developed a holy scripture that is their own.

Rastafarians have managed to influence the general Caribbean society to some extent through their music and dress. The "dreadlocks" hairstyle that is worn by some Rastafarians is very popular and has become a merchandising point throughout the world. The jargon of the Rastafarian—"I man" and "Irie"—is now established in the Jamaican vernacular. Rastafarianism is a subculture that is here to stay.

More recently, the subculture of "posse groups" or "Jamaican posses" has gained attention. The drug-pushing, gang warfare, and generally disorderly conduct of these groups have made them a concern for correctional and law enforcement practitioners in the United States. These posses are highly organized and have a hierarchical organizational structure. The culture of these groups does not have any strong, recognizable connection to traditional West Indian or Jamaican culture. However, some groups use symbols from indigenous superstitions beliefs (Voodoo and Obeah) to intimidate their potential victims.

Many posse members embrace Rastafarianism on the superficial level of wearing red, green, and gold colors and sporting dreadlocks. Many of their members are called "ball heads" because they maintain traditional dress and hair styles. The percentage of individuals involved in this type of activity is small in comparison with the Jamaican population. These groups are now beginning to have an effect on the Jamaican community because of their violence and drug pushing. The activities of these groups violate the cultural norms and values that are practiced by the mainstream community in Jamaica and the West Indians.

More recently, the correctional system has began to focus on West Indians because of an increase in their presence within the system. There is a strong tendency to stereotype all West Indians as being Jamaican. The influx of Jamaicans into the correctional system in this country is significant in comparison to the other Caribbean islands. This increase has been due primarily to drug-related crimes and illegal immigration status. However, the assumption should not be made that all Caribbean Islanders are Jamaicans and have identical cultural traits.

# Conclusion

For correctional practitioners to have effective cross-cultural interaction, it is important to recognize that Caribbean Islanders (West Indians) are products of a dynamic, creative, and forceful heritage. Cultural experiences vary throughout the Caribbean islands. West Indians can be aggressive, but when accorded the dignity and respect they deserve, they are a docile group of people.

West Indians' perceptions about the correctional system in the United States are markedly different from that which they hold for the system in each Caribbean island. The U. S. correctional system is seen as one where justice is swift and fast, highly organized, and does not allow room for bribery. In dealing with West Indians in a correctional environment, this perception can be beneficial for effectively understanding and dealing with this group of people.

# Reference

Jamaica Information Service. 1973. *The official handbook of Jamaica*. Kingston, Jamaica: J.I.S.

# 5. Islam in America's Prisons

*By Matthew B. Hamidullah*

Islam is not a new religion. The fundamental and most essential belief of Islam is the belief in one all-powerful, all-wise, living God. This belief in the unity of God (Tawhid) is the very essence of Islam and the starting point for the Muslim. Allah is the Arabic name for God and is used by Arabic-speaking Christians and Muslims. The second part of the belief of Muslims is the profession of faith, which is an affirmation of Muhammad as the messenger of Allah, the last and final prophet, who serves as a model for the Muslim community. Muhammad was not divine, but a human being. He is the model husband, father, leader, and judge and an excellent example in all human endeavors.

For one fifth of the world's population (over one billion people), Islam is both a religion and a way of life. The Arabic word "Islam" means submission and derives its meaning from a word meaning peace. In a religious context, it means complete submission to the will of God (Allah). A Muslim is one who believes in Allah and submits his or her will to the will of Allah.

Mohammadanism is thus a misnomer and is offensive to Muslims because it suggests that Muslims worship Muhammad rather than Allah. When asked what is Islam, the Prophet of Allah, in an authentic tradition said, "It is to bear witness that there is none worthy of worship except Allah and to bear witness that Muhammad is the messenger of Allah, to establish formal prayer (Salat), to pay the poor tax (Zakat), to fast during the month of Ramadhan, and to make pilgrimage (Hajj) to Mecca at least once is one's lifetime, if one can afford it." The structure of Islam is built on these five pil-

*Matthew B. Hamidullah is the religious services administrator for the Mid-Atlantic Region of the Federal Bureau of Prisons, Annapolis Junction, Md. His duty station is the Federal Correctional Institution at Butner, North Carolina.*

lars: (1) Iman (faith) in God and reciting the Kalimah (principle of faith), (2) to establish Salat (prayer), (3) to pay the Zakat (poor tax), (4) to fast during the month of Ramadhan, and (5) to perform Hajj (pilgrimage) to Mecca.

Iman is proclaiming the Kalimah with the tongue and to affirm the truth of this principle in one's heart and with one's actions. Profession of this principle of faith in Islam requires that one believes in the following Articles of Faith:

1. Allah is the one and only creator, sustainer, lord of all the worlds. This belief means that the Muslim accepts that Allah is the all-knowing, that Allah has absolute control over all aspects of life, that Allah is the sole governor of life and death, and that He shares His rule with no one. The Muslim believes that Allah has no partners or equals and that He is the sole dispenser of mercy, justice, peace, and love.

2. The angels of Allah are pure, spiritual, unseen creatures who are constantly devoting their existence to Allah and executing all the commands of Allah without any capacity to disobey.

3. The prophets (messengers) of Allah are divinely inspired men who devoted their lives to the mission of conveying the message of Allah to the nations of the world. A Muslim must believe in all the prophets of Allah, including Adam, Noah, Abraham, Moses, Jesus, and Muhammad.

4. The books of Allah are the words of Allah revealed to the prophets in their original form. Muslims believe that none of these books remain in their original form except the Holy Qur'an. The Qur'an is therefore viewed by Muslims as the criteria by which the previous books are judged.

5. The day of judgment is when all humankind will be brought back to life (physically and spiritually), and each person must give an account for the conscious acts of his or her life. The Muslim believes that no burden bearer can bear the burden of another. The persons who maintained their belief and lived a righteous life will have eternal bliss in paradise. Those persons who rebelled

against Allah in His rule or those who associated someone or something with Allah will be punished and will
suffer condemnation in the hell-fire.

6. The destiny is acceptance of Allah's will (good and bad
fate) as it affects one's life.


Muslims look first to the Holy Qur'an, which contains Allah's
commands, and second to the example (sunnah) of the prophet
Muhammad, who serves as the embodiment of Islamic values, as a
living model for the Muslim community. Traditions or reports
(Hadiths) of Prophet Muhammad's words and deeds were preserved
and written down by early Muslim communities. On the basis of
Qur'an and Sunnah, the Islamic way of life was developed and
codified comprehensively in the Shariah—Islamic law. It is an
obligation for all Muslims to follow the Shariah.

# Characteristics of Islamic Ideology

Islam has no mythology. The teachings of Islam are simple and ra-
tional. The religion is free from superstitions and illogical beliefs.
There is no hierarchy of priests or complicated rites and rituals. The
criteria for leadership in Islam include knowledge of the Qur'an,
knowledge of Hadith (sayings of the Prophet), excellence of character, seniority of acceptance of Islam, and seniority of age. Muslims
meet and select leaders, who then become the spokesmen for the
group after they have decided their affairs by mutual consultation.
Prophet Muhammad always encouraged the Muslims to select a
leader. The Prophet stated: "If there are three of you on a journey,
then select a leader." Muslims are ordered in the Holy Qur'an "to
obey Allah, obey His messengers and obey those in authority over
them." Everyone may approach the Book of Allah directly and
translate its directives into practice. Islam encourages each believer
to excel in life. All Muslims are taught to value education and learning. The Prophet of Islam said:

He who leaves his home in search of knowledge walks in
the path of God.

To seek knowledge is obligatory for every Muslim.

Acquire knowledge, because he who acquires it in the way of the Lord performs an act of piety, he who disseminates it bestows alms, and he who imparts it to others performs an act of devotion to Allah (Khurshid 1989).

This emphasis on learning is the manner in which Islam seeks to bring humanity out of a world of ignorance and superstition. Learning and teaching are given a premium in Islam.

Islam promotes belief and practice. Righteous conduct must follow belief in Allah. The religion is something to be lived and not an act of mere profession of faith. The Qur'an says: "For those who believe and work righteousness is every blessedness, and a beautiful place of final return" (Qur'an 13:29). Prophet Muhammad said: "God does not accept belief, if it is not expressed in deeds and does not accept deeds if they do not conform to belief."

Islam does not compartmentalize life into a spiritual world and a material world. In Islam, human existence and behavior are one. Islam does not permit any separation in moral and material life or spiritual and mundane life. Islam focuses on establishing a balance between spiritual and material demands of life. Islam seeks to foster the idea that everything in this world is for the benefit of humanity; while humanity's purpose is to establish a moral and just world so that all humankind may fulfill/obey the will of God. Islam, then, provides its followers with an integrated, holistic way of life that was revealed by Allah to all the prophets from the time of Abraham to Muhammad, one final time, and recorded in the Holy Qur'an.

Islam is a complete way of life. It provides guidance for all walks of life: individual and social, material and religious, legal and political, financial and cultural, national and international. Islam also endeavors to establish a balance between the individual and society. Islam guarantees basic human rights while at the same time promoting a sense of social responsibility in the individual for the collective good. Islam encourages social life as the expression of the higher order of life, with an emphasis placed on collective acts of worship: congregational prayers, the giving of alms, and the performance of the pilgrimage to Mecca.

Islam does not promote or recognize nationalism. The teachings of Islam are universal and benefit all humankind. The religion is equally applicable to all people in all regions of the world and for all times. Islam promotes allegiance to values and places little emphasis on allegiance to nations. Islam is void of any emphasis on race and/or color, with regard to the value of a human being. Excellence is measured by one's conviction and behavior, not by the color of one's skin. The Qur'an says: ''Among God's signs are the creation of the heavens and of the earth and the diversity of your languages and of your colors. In this indeed are signs for those who know'' (Qur'an 30:22). The Qur'an also says: ''O mankind! We have created you from a single soul, male and female, and made you into nations and tribes, so that you may come to know one another. Truly, the most honored of you in God's sight is the greatest of you in piety. God is all-knowing, all-aware'' (Qur'an 49:13). It is clear that the Qur'an expresses no support for racial or color prejudice. In Islam, piety is more important than birthplace, national ties, or aristocratic interest.

The issue of color-consciousness in Islam is also addressed in *The Autobiography of Malcolm X* (Malcolm X & Haley 1966). Malcolm X made the following observation during his pilgrimage to Mecca, which coincided with his separation from the Nation of Islam:

> The color blindness of the Muslim world's religious society and the color blindness of the Muslim's world's human society; these two influences had each day been making a greater impact, and an interesting persuasion against any previous way of thinking. . .

> There were tens of thousands of pilgrims, from all over the world. They were of all colours, from blue-eyed blondes to black-skinned Africans. But we were all participating in the same ritual, displaying a spirit of unity and brotherhood that my experiences in America had led me to believe never could exist between the white and the non-white (Malcom X & Haley 1966).

Malcolm X's thoughts show that he believed Islam is not a religion based on color. No Muslim self-identifies with the color of one's skin as a basis for identification. Therefore, terms such as Black Muslims or White Muslims are offensive and an anathema in the realm of Islam. It is sufficient to say Muslim when referring to an adherent of Islam.

Forty-two percent of the nearly six million Muslims in America are African Americans. A very small percentage of the Muslims incarcerated in U.S. prisons are non-African-American. Because a disproportionate number of African Americans are incarcerated in U.S. prisons, it would be logical to conclude that the majority of Muslims in U.S. prisons would be African American. A significant number of the Muslims incarcerated have converted to Islam while in prison through invitations to attend meetings that are, for the most part, inmate-led. This contributes to the perception that the religion is a "black religion."

Another passage from *The Autobiography of Malcolm X* focuses on the issue of people grouping together based on a common knowledge or interest.

> There was a color pattern in the huge crowds. Once I happened to notice this, I closely observed it thereafter. Being from America made me intensely sensitive to matters of color. I saw that people who looked alike drew together and most of the time stayed together. This was entirely voluntary; there being no other reason for it. But Africans were with Africans, Pakistanis were with Pakistanis. And so on. I tucked it into my mind that when I returned home I would tell Americans this observation; that where true brotherhood existed among all colors, where no one felt segregated, where there was no "superiority" complex, no "inferiority" complex—then voluntarily, naturally, people of the same kind felt drawn together by that which they had in common. . . (Malcom X & Haley 1966).

# Practicing Islam in Prison

## *Prayer (Salat)*

Muslims are required to make formal prayers (Salat) five times within a twenty-four-hour period everyday. Salat has been commanded eighty-two times in the Holy Qur'an, with specific instructions: "When ye pass congregational prayers, celebrate God's praises, standing, sitting down, or lying on your sides; but when ye are free from danger, set up regular prayers: for such prayers are enjoined on believers at stated times" (Qur'an 4:103). The five times of prayers are as follows:

- *dawn prayer*—offered at the first break of day before sunrise

- *noon prayer*—offered between midday (after the sun begins to decline from its zenith) and before the time for the mid-afternoon prayer

- *mid-afternoon prayer*—offered midway between the time for the noon prayer and sunset (when the shadow of an object begins to exceed its length)

- *sunset prayer*—offered immediately after the sun sets up to the disappearance of the red glow of the twilight

- *night prayer*—offered anytime after the disappearance of the red glow in the western sky and before the dawn prayer (preferably this prayer is said before midnight)

Any of the prayers may be performed individually; however, it is desirable for Muslims to pray collectively whenever possible. The prayers can generally be said in ten to fifteen minutes. For the prayers to be valid, the following conditions must be met:

1. The person must perform an ablution (washing of hands, face, arms, head, mouth, and feet in clean running water). Following a wet dream or any seminal emission, a full ceremonial bath/shower (ghusl) must be taken. Muslims use the sinks in the bathrooms to wash their feet as part of the ablutions. Ceremonial ablutions are prerequisites to the prayers. A person who has not performed the necessary ablutions will not be permitted to sit on the prayer rugs.

2. A person must be in clothes that are free of blood, urine, or any other impurities. Women on their menses are exempt from performing their daily prayers until they have completely stopped bleeding. It is permissible for non-

Muslims to be present during the prayers. Muslims do not pray to the east or to the sun, but toward the Ka'ba in Mecca. The Ka'ba is the stone house of worship in Mecca that Allah commanded Abraham and Ismail to build over 4,000 years ago.

3. The place of prayer must be clean and free of all impurities, including statues or images of animals or humans. Music is not permitted during prayer times.

## Jum'ah Prayer/Friday Prayer

At midday on Friday, Muslims observe a service ordained in the Holy Qur'an: "Oh you who believe! When the call is proclaimed to prayer on Friday (the day of Assembly) hasten to the remembrance earnestly of Allah and leave off business, that is best for you if you but knew" (Qur'an 62:9-10). This prayer service takes the place of the afternoon prayer on Fridays, and it must be said in congregation. The Friday midday prayer is not valid unless it is said in congregation. Muslims may work before and after the Jum'ah prayer services. There is no religious requirement that would exempt anyone from not working on Friday.

Following a sermon (khutbah), which can cover any aspect of life of the Muslim community, the prayer is said. The sermon is said in two parts. A minimum of one hour should be provided for the Friday prayer service. The Muslims will make a call to prayer and sit quietly on the floor in preparation for the prayer service. Prayer rugs will be used by the worshippers. The Imam or prayer leader will use a chair to sit in before and during the break in between the two parts of the sermon. A rostrum may also be used by the prayer leader.

Muslims use prayer oils/fragrances during the prayers in keeping with the traditions of Prophet Muhammad. The Prophet said: "Take a bath on Friday and wash your heads," meaning take a thorough bath and use perfume. The Prophet also said, "The taking of a bath on Friday is compulsory for every male Muslim who has attained the age of puberty and (also) the cleaning of his teeth with miswak and the using of perfume if it is available." Miswak is a wooden tooth stick from a particular tree in the Middle East that is used for cleaning the teeth prior to prayer and when one gets up. This implement is approximately five inches in length and the width of a pencil. Muslims will also use prayer beads, which are used to remember the names of Allah. Muslim prayer beads are similar to Catholic rosary beads.

Muslims should bathe on Friday before the service. The bath does not occur just before the prayer service but any time from late Thursday night to early Friday morning. Participating in work detail does not automatically require another shower before the Jum'ah prayer service. If one's clothing is filthy, or if there is a strong body odor, one should be allowed to bathe and change clothes. A pat search by a correctional officer (male or female) does not automatically invalidate the ceremonial purity of the worshipper. From a religious standpoint, the touching violates the separation of the sexes, but not the ablution.

A male Muslim must cover his private parts, which are from his navel to his knees. The private parts of female Muslims are their whole bodies except their feet, hands, and face. Muslim men may want to wear turbans and long shirts to the knee or ankle during the prayer services. Prophet Muhammad wore a kufi (a small cap that usually fits flush on the head) and a turban most of the time, as did his companions. Many Muslim men continue this practice of covering the head. A kufi may be any color. Muslim women cover their heads at all times. Muslim women will also wish to wear clothing that covers their bodies.

## Fasting during Ramadhan

Ramadhan is the ninth month on the lunar calendar. It begins with the sighting of the new moon and ends with the sighting of the new moon of the next month. The month of Ramadhan consists of twenty-nine or thirty days. The lunar calendar of the Muslims is 354 days in length; therefore Ramadhan moves up approximately eleven days each year in the Roman calendar. The fast of Ramadhan begins at dawn (approximately an hour and forty minutes before sunrise) and ends at sunset. The fast is a religious obligation; it is not voluntary. Ramadhan is a total devotional religious rite, not merely abstention from food and drink. The fast is a pillar of the Muslim's faith in Allah and is performed in conjunction with the pillars of Salat and Zakat. The Holy Qur'an is read during this month and the devotees seek the pleasure of Allah. Ramadhan is not a time for dieting and has no significance to anyone other than a Muslim.

Any person who is insane, traveling, suffering from an illness, or any woman on her menses or pregnant is exempted from the fast as long as these conditions prevail. The days missed are to be made up at a later time. The fast is a complete abstention from all foods, liquids, medicine, tobacco, sexual relations (ejaculations of any type), and the use of profanity during fasting hours. Fasting Muslims must also refrain from getting angry. Injections do not break the fast, whether they are for feeding the person or for administering medication.

A precondition for eating the evening meal is drinking water, eating dried fruit (preferably dates), and performing the sunset prayers. A light morning meal is consumed before dawn. Fasting Muslims observe the ''Night of Power.'' This is the night that the initial revelations from the Holy Qur'an were revealed to Prophet Muhammad. Muslims gather for night prayer vigils throughout the evening on the Night of Power. The Night of Power can be observed on any of the odd-number nights during the last ten nights of the month of Ramadhan. The twenty-seventh and twenty-ninth nights of Ramadhan are the preferred nights for the observance. Muslims observe a three-day period of Islamic celebration (Eid-ul-Fitr) at the conclusion of Ramadhan.

## Dietary Laws of Islam

The Holy Qur'an says: ''What Allah has made lawful in His Book is Halal (lawful) and what he has forbidden is Haram (sinful)'' (Qur'an 19:64). ''Forbidden to you are the flesh of dead animals (that die on their own) and blood and the flesh of swine and that which has been dedicated to any other God than Allah'' (Qur'an 5:3-4). Seafood is exempt from the restriction of eating dead flesh. Muslims are forbidden to use any pork or pork by-products. This includes handling of pork in any fashion. Alcohol is not permitted. Muslims have a required ritual slaughter of meat, which involves reciting the name of God over the animal and cutting the animal's neck, so that the blood can drain freely from the animal. The Prophet of Islam taught that ''. . . your body has rights over you,'' and the consumption of wholesome food and the leading of a healthy lifestyle are seen as religious obligations.

## Islamic Holy Days

Muslims observe two high holy day periods annually; one in connection with the completion of Ramadhan and the other in association with the pilgrimage to Mecca. These festival periods last three days. The festivals are as follows:

1. Eid-ul-Fitr is the feast of the breaking of the fast. This festival is observed on the first morning after the end of the fasting rites of Ramadhan.

2. Eid-ul-Adha is the feast of sacrifice. This festival is observed on the morning of the tenth day of the month of Dhul-Hijjah on the Islamic lunar calendar. It falls approximately seventy days after Ramadhan.

Both festivals involve a prayer service that should be said on the morning of the day indicated. The prayer should be said as soon as possible after sunrise and must be said before noon. It is Islamic tradition to eat an odd number of dates before going to the Eid prayer of Eid-ul-Fitr. One should not eat anything until returning from the Eid-ul-Adha.

The service in scope and nature is very similar to the Friday Jum'ah prayer service, except the prayers are said before the sermon. The service generally concludes within an hour. The same requirements for Jum'ah prayer regarding clothing, bathing, oils, etc., are in effect for the Eid prayer services. A ceremonial meal is held in conjunction with the two festival periods.

## The Muslim Marriage

A Muslim marriage is not a sacrament, but a simple, legal agreement/contract in which either party is free to include conditions. A hadith (saying of the Prophet) regarding marriage is, ''When a man marries he has fulfilled half of the religion, so let him fear Allah regarding the remaining half.'' A marriage dowry is given by the groom to the bride for her personal use, and she may keep her family name. Although frowned upon, divorce is not forbidden. The

Prophet said, "The lawful thing which Allah hates most is divorce."

## Death and Dying in Islam

When a person is facing imminent death, it is extremely important that an Imam (religious leader) in the community be notified. The Imam will perform the last rites, encouraging the dying Muslim to recite: "There is nothing worthy of worship except Allah and Muhammad is the Messenger of Allah" and verses from the Holy Qur'an. The Imam will spend time praying with the dying. At the point of death, the person should be placed with his or her head facing toward the Ka'ba in Mecca and put on his or her right side if at all possible. Normally, Muslims do not perform autopsies on the deceased. Burial occurs within twenty-four hours without embalming the body. Care should be exercised when notifying the family of the deceased Muslim concerning autopsies and embalming.

## Name Changes

There is no requirement for a person to change their name when accepting Islam. There is a saying of Prophet Muhammad, which encourages Muslims to be called by the best names. Many Muslims choose names from Allah's attributes or names that reflect their Islamic way of life.

# Conclusion

Islam emphasizes the belief in one God and encourages Muslims to conform their lives to obey the commandments of their Lord. Islam is one of the fastest-growing religions in America and will continue to have a growing influence as America becomes more culturally diverse.

It is virtually impossible to generalize about American Muslims or Islam in the prisons of America. Islam continues to attract people from many walks of life. Muslims arrived early in America and have made a significant impact on the social and cultural landscape. Islam is a vibrant force in the prisons of America. It is particularly attractive to people who are searching for a sense of oneness of God, humankind, and purpose. Islam may seem strange or even extreme in this modern world. Islam, unlike some western religions, dominates the life of the Muslim. Islam is always the determining factor in the decision-making process of the Muslim. For the Muslim, there is no distinction between secular and religious life. Muslims believe in the Divine Law of Allah, the Shari'a. It is critical that correctional workers understand the intensity of belief of the Muslims and develop an appreciation of their diversity of faith.

# References

Khurshid, A. 1989. *Islam: Basic principles and characteristics.* Plainfield, Indiana: American Trust Publications.

Malcom X and A. Haley. 1966. *The Autobiography of Malcolm X.* New York: Grove Press.

# 6. Hispanic Culture

*By Orlando L. Martinez*

The purpose of this chapter is to provide corrections planners, policy makers, and practitioners better understanding of Hispanic culture. This understanding may lead to specific strategies for use on a practical level. Significant to understanding cultural and ethnic differences of Hispanics is language and family, especially how they pertain to human behavior and human experience. Hispanic inmates will be best served if adequate assessment processes are developed that identify the multiple factors that need to be considered in addressing security and treatment decisions.

## Culture

Culture may be described as the collective conscious and unconscious of a group of people who share the same ethnicity. People are products of their culture and geographic environments, family group, local setting, regional identity, national identity and experience, and social situation. They are also influenced by the particular ways in which cultural issues, such as territoriality, discrimination, institutional oppression, and normative behavior, have shaped their lives. Certain themes, images, beliefs and their expression are at the heart of culture. The modes individuals of a particular ethnic group use to respond, react, problem solve, and cope with the community and with each other is what comprises culture.

## Language

Although all human groups have these images, both conscious and unconscious, Vega (1989) argues that it is the "idiosyncratic"

---

*Orlando L. Martinez is a corrections consultant in Highlands Ranch, Colorado.*

nature or expression of these collective imagery symbolisms that is uniquely owned by a particular ethnic group that makes it different. The constellation of life issues, large and small, such as health practices, child rearing, sexuality, and self-adornment, are framed in a particular way that is unique. Moreover, researchers have described language as the medium through which interpretation of these daily transactions is conducted (Vega 1989). Although not all ethnic or racial groups have a language unto themselves (e.g., Hispanics), language nuances among groups have long been recognized (National Coalition 1989). In a subgroup, such as Mexican-American youth, individuals may use particular words and physical expressions, such as handshakes, that may not be recognizable or even acceptable outside their particular milieu or reference group. Thus, communication becomes one vehicle that admits or does not admit individuals or groups into an ethnic or cultural interaction (Constantino et al. 1986).

An example of this is humor. Ethnic humor has a special place in the hearts and minds of ethnic groups because it exploits experiences or events common to that group in a unique way. Not long ago a friend of mine was sitting in a small group chatting about food when one person mentioned a particular soup common among Southwest Mexican Americans. To those who ate it as a child or do so now, the "magical" power of this soup is folklore. Thus, jokes made about the medicinal use of this soup were found to be funny among the Mexican Americans in the room who have shared this common food/experience. Others in the room "did not get it" when the punch lines were given out.

In settings where different languages are used, humor can be easily missed if one does not speak the language—often if the joke is translated, it fails. Thus some images encoded in language cannot be adequately translated. The image or message is culturally specific.

# The Family

On the average, Hispanics have large families because of their religious beliefs and social traditions. Because most Hispanics are Catholic, they tend to practice less birth control than non-Catholics. Moreover, because many come from traditional rural societies, many preserve personal feelings that require having children to feel truly masculine or feminine. Also, poverty, rural or urban, tends to encourage the use of children as breadwinners.

As compared generally with Anglo-Americans, authority and tradition are powerful forces among Hispanics. There is little doubt that the husband is the head of the family. Publicly, at least, he must appear to have control over his children and wife. A good wife may well be defined by the skill with which she deals with the authority of her husband. From childhood, sex roles assign a dominant position to the boy and a subordinate one to the girl.

Therefore, a woman's influence, although very great, is expressed through personal dealings with her husband rather than through a challenge to his authority. Commonly, the husband gives great latitude to the wife to manage the house, raise the children, and spend the income. Many Hispanic husbands avoid child-rearing to the point that they foster independence in their wives and children. The mother commonly receives the intense love of her children, while the father is given respect as a provider and a keeper of the peace.

Great demands and pressure from outside the Hispanic community have made the family all the more critical for survival. Outside influences often strain family cohesiveness. Discrimination, poverty, violence, and loneliness of the uprooted minority create feelings that can sometimes only be expressed among family members. In such circumstances, fathers may abandon the family or abuse their wives and children, siblings may grow apart, and so forth. On the whole, the basic strength of authority and tradition has endured such threats. Among Hispanics, the family continues to be a haven from the often hostile Anglo world of work or school. Relatives and family friends tend to stick together more than other families that have the freedom stemming from economic comfort and social acceptance.

The function of the family is crucial to Hispanics, but family influence can be harmful in dealing with the outside Anglo majority. In schools, work, society, and politics, where other values dominate, what the Hispanic child learns at home poses problems he or she cannot always solve. For example, learning respect for others can pose problems in a society that often rewards being outspoken and blunt, if not rude. Learning as a cooperative spirit among family and friends does not prepare one for schools where aggressive and competitive conduct is assumed to win the prize of academic or social prestige.

In terms of Anglo-American social values that are closely linked to movement, progress, energy, aggressiveness, and social change, the Hispanic family tradition appears to be a handicap.

# Cross-cultural Assessment

Because culture is dynamic, changing, and reflective, it is important to understand processes of culture if one is to successfully interact with Hispanics. If each generation of a cultural group is viewed as one passenger car on a long train moving across a plain, each age group would move across this plain at a different point in time, and thus the "landscape" that one saw toward the end of the train might be somewhat changed from that which the passenger at the front of the train viewed. The point is that culture being fluid and reflective may be difficult to transfer to youth in a way that accurately reflects the values and principles of their parents and elders.

What is known about cultural and ethnic groups is known only for any given time and place. Assessment is one way to determine what is going on with people at a certain point in time. The following variables should be examined during assessment:

- original and current national identity
- original and current regional identity
-  original and current local identity
- rural and urban experiences
- generational identity
- social class
- economic status
- racism and discrimination experienced
- sexism experienced
- subsystems, such as the education and religion with which the person is involved

These factors relate to behavior people learn as members and participants in larger cultural systems and through which assessments can be made about where people have been and what experiences they have had that have influenced their behavior, their concepts of expected or "ideal" behavior, and their ideas about expressing behavior derived from their experiences in their cultural subsystems. The idea is to provide a framework within which steps taken in assessment can be systematically organized into a process that identifies means of effective intervention.

# Cross-ethnic Assessment

Ethnicity refers to further cultural distinctiveness. People are members of ethnic groups and therefore have both individual and group-related identity, experiences, and social realities. Their special reference group provides them with traditions, a reference language, and other variables connected with a unique set of behaviors. This is an experience shared with others but interpreted by each individual and therefore does not result in a class of people or an ethnic group whose members think, act, and believe alike. Furthermore, the group is not static. Many facets of ethnicity need to be examined when undertaking assessment:

- reference group identity, which involves the extent to which the person identifies with his or her ethnic group
- self-identification, or what the person calls himself or herself
- group identification, or what the person's group is called
- given name and name changes
- intermarriage and its influence on the person's adherence to the traditions of his or her ethnic group
- traditional behavior, which includes behavior relating to language and communication; roles, such as those of females, males, children, and other family members; family systems; rituals, ceremonies, and customs; informal systems; folk medicine and similar

systems; and symbols of identity, such as clothes that identify the individual as a member of a particular group

- values, which include the person's cultural, political, and spiritual values and the values that have historically belonged to his or her ethnic group

Ethnicity represents an awareness, a sense of in-group identity, whether this identity is valued or accepted or not. It provides the individual with continuity with his or her past and with a sense of belonging to a people, a history, and a specific culture. This consciousness can also be a bond, an image, or a symbol related to ethnic values, depending on the significance it carries for the person.

Finally, it should be noted that the cultural and ethnic experience of Hispanics and other minorities involves the major elements of dualism and survival behavior as well as the element of identity. Identity is both cultural and ethnic and is learned, dynamic, and changing. Dealing with the simultaneous attraction to group and larger society means that the individual needs to develop coping skills as well as a sense of being someone who interacts with two worlds.

Corrections planners, policy makers, and practitioners must recognize and respect the cultural diversity of their clients and the community at large. Accordingly, we must provide services in appropriate cultural contexts and further our understanding of different behaviors, traditions, and life experiences both within the workforce and client population. Good policy and practice requires organizations to become culturally competent and literate so that positive cross-cultural experiences can be provided to correctional clients in the most appropriate security and treatment setting.

# References

Constantino, M., and R. Constantino. 1986. *Journal of Consulting and Clinical Psychology* 54(5).

National Coalition of Hispanic Health and Human Services Organizations. 1988. *Delivering preventive health care to*

*Hispanics: A manual for providers.* Washington, D.C.: COSSMHO.

Vega, W. A. 1989. *What is a culturally sensitive prevention program?* Miami: University of Miami.

# 7. American Indians: Criminal Justice and Stereotyping

*By Carol Chiago Lujan, Ph.D.*

Stereotyping is an insidious form of oppression that has persisted in Euroamerica's perceptions of American Indians for centuries. The stereotypes of American Indians range from the image of the noble savage to the ignoble savage. These exaggerated beliefs of American Indians are perpetuated through various means, including mass media, schools, literature, and film. Unfortunately, the stereotypes persist and can be seen in the discriminatory treatment of American Indians in the criminal justice system.

The term American Indian rather than Native American is primarily used here because the term Native American is too broad in its definition. For example, the term Native American could conceivably be applied to such people as native Hawaiians and any person born in America. Whereas the term American Indian is more specific and refers to the nations and individuals that are indigenous to the continental United States and have experienced, in common, the early assimilative and paternalistic policies of the United States government.

## Stereotypes and American Indians

Stereotypes are an important component in the development and maintenance of prejudice. Burkey (1978) has two categories of stereotypes: conflict racism, where the individual/group is viewed as

*Carol Chiago Lujan, Ph.D., is a member of the Navajo Nation and an assistant professor in the School of Justice Studies at Arizona State University in Tempe.*

threatening, and paternalistic racism, where the individual/group is viewed as dependent. If the group is viewed as threatening, members of the group are likely to be perceived as treacherous savages. If the group is viewed as dependent, members are likely to be perceived as primitive and childlike. Additional factors contribute to the perpetuation of stereotypes of American Indians, including the distorted historical account of American Indians and the misconceptions about their political and economic standing.

The American Indian has been portrayed as noble savage and ignoble savage, depending on the period in history. As the situation changes, the image of the American Indian also changes. The trend in the 1990s is to portray both images of the noble and the ignoble savage. This "good Indian-bad Indian" theme can be seen in popular films such as *Dances With Wolves*, *Thunderheart*, and *Last of the Mohicans*.

Deloria (1980) discusses the attitudinal changes of Indians based on their perceived threat in the following account by John Smith in his description of the Powhatan Indians in the early 1600s:

> The first testimony by western Europeans visiting the American continent saw the inhabitants as "happy, gentle people.... They traded kindly with me and my men," .... Twenty years later, when the colonists had pushed the Indians into war, Smith described them as "beasts, a viperous brood, hellhounds and miscreants." Savages they were only in their resistance to exploitation, but the image stuck and was reinforced whenever and wherever the two races met.

The prevailing attitude among the American Indians is that they have been intentionally stereotyped by Euroamericans to justify and legitimize the exploitation and oppression of native people.

Wilkinson (1974) argues that the images of the drunken, dumb, helpless savage, as well as the image of the noble savage who is detached from reality, reinforce Euroamerica's concept of its own superiority and at the same time work to destroy the self-concept of the American Indian. According to Wilkinson, "The media has, for its own purposes, created a false image of the Native American (sic). Too many of us have patterned ourselves after that image. It is time that we project our own image and stop being what we never really were.''

Freire (1985) helps to accentuate this concern:

> ...The invaders penetrate the cultural context of another group, in disrespect of the latter's potentialities; they impose their own view of the world upon those they invade and inhibit the creativity of the invaded by curbing their expression. Cultural invasion is thus always an act of violence against the persons of the invaded culture, who lose their originality or face the threat of losing it.

Various explanations have been presented regarding the discriminatory manner in which American Indians are treated within the criminal justice system. Many of these explanations center on racist stereotyping and labeling, paternalism, and language and cultural factors (Zatz, Lujan & Snyder-Joy 1991). The two areas that appear to be most significant on the processing of Indians within the justice system are racial stereotyping and cultural and language factors.

# Stereotype of the Drunken Indian

Because of the negative stereotyping of American Indians that has been perpetuated throughout the centuries in the literature and media, many American Indians accept the negative stereotype about themselves. Nowhere is this self-acceptance of the negative stereotype more evident than in the image of the ''drunken Indian.'' In a survey on the Navajo reservation, 63 percent of the Navajos interviewed believed that Indians were biologically predisposed to alcohol (May & Smith 1988).

Research to date does not indicate that American Indians are different from other people regarding the physiology of alcohol metabolism (Bennion & Li 1976; Farris & Jones 1978; Fenna et al. 1971; Schaefer 1981; Zeiner, Paredes & Cowden 1976). Despite the lack of scientific evidence to support the notion of a physiological or biological predisposition to alcohol, the myth prevails.

Because of the negative stereotyping of American Indians as alcoholics, both Indian and non-Indian people may have distorted and negative views regarding alcohol. The perpetuation of this stereotype makes Indians more vulnerable to alcohol-related arrests (Stewart 1964). The relationship between alcohol and crime among American Indians has been discussed in a number of studies. Stratton (1973) found that alcohol-related offenses accounted for 85 percent to 90 percent of all arrests of Indians in Gallup, New Mexico, in 1969. Many police officers in this study held the view that all Indians who drink are drunks or that Indians are racially unable to drink moderately. Levy, Kunitz, and Everett's (1969) analysis on Navajo homicide and alcohol found minimal differences between the Navajo rates when compared with data collected in Philadelphia.

The cursory review of research on American Indians and alcohol presented here suggests that the "drunken Indian" stereotype may be a factor in determining whether or not an American Indian is processed through the judicial system. There also appears to be little difference in American Indian alcohol-related crimes when compared to non-Indians. In addition, issues of class and culture may be as important as alcohol relative to crime and American Indians.

# Culture and Language

The literature indicates the critical influence of language and cultural differences in the criminal justice process. The demeanor, dress, and attitude of American Indians many times differ from that of the majority population and can be misinterpreted as negative (Bynum & Paternoster 1984; Feimer, Pommersheim & Wise 1990; Pommersheim & Wise 1989; Hall & Simkus 1975; Weber 1982). For example, because of religious beliefs and traditions, many Indian men continue to wear their hair long. This often creates negative perceptions by non-Indian officials, both in the educational system and the criminal justice system (Zatz, Lujan & Snyder-Joy 1991).

Although many tribes now have courts that resemble the Euroamerican judicial system, these court proceedings are usually less formal than the non-Indian courts and are composed of Indian people (i.e., judges, attorneys, and juries). In addition, tribal courts are more likely to rely on restitution-oriented solutions than punitive outcomes. Non-Indian courts differ in that they are more formal and are highly unlikely to have American Indians serving as jurors or judicial officials.

Language is another critical factor in court proceedings. It is not uncommon for American Indian first-time offenders to plead guilty. Although tribal courts tend to replicate the Euroamerican court system, they are more humanistic and less formal in structure and content. Tribal members are usually acquainted with members of the tribal court and are somewhat familiar with its proceedings. Furthermore, there have been a number of cases where due to language differences, mitigating and/or extenuating circumstances that would have resulted in less severe treatment were not presented until after the individual had been convicted and sentenced. Currently many courts are relying on translators to assist in the court proceedings. However, some courts, such as the U. S. District courts, do not allow enough time for adequate translation. For a number of American Indian languages, such as Navajo, it is difficult to translate certain words and concepts that are commonly used in judicial proceedings. For example, in the Navajo language there is no concept for the word "hypothetical." Yet this is a word frequently used in the courts.

# Research on Criminal Justice and American Indians

A seminal study on sentencing by Hall and Simkus (1975) highlights the unequal treatment of American Indians in the criminal justice system. This comparative study found that Indians were 8 percent more likely than whites to be convicted of felonies and twice as likely as their white counterparts to serve time in prison. Hall and Simkus present several reasons for this unequal treatment: negative stereotyping and labeling, more visibility outside the reservation, the social and economic conflict with the white community, and inability to hire effective lawyers and to plea negotiations.

Hall and Simkus conclude that American Indians may be punished more severely because of who and what they are rather than what they have done. They suggest that the criminal justice personnel's negative stereotype of the Indian reservation as a welfare state suffering from disorganization may have a significant effect on the court's decisions in terms of the type of sentence given. "It is possible that the reservation environment is perceived by some judges as much less conducive to successful completion of a probationary term, making the native American offender a poor 'risk' for the judicial system" (Hall & Simkus 1975).

Hall and Simkus substantiate earlier findings of discrimination by Stewart (1964), Riffenburgh (1964), and Stratton (1973). A similar study by Swift and Bickel (1974) found that Indians received longer sentences than whites within the federal system. However, a study by Bynum and Paternoster (1984) found that non-Indians received longer sentences than Indians. Studies by Pommersheim and Wise (1989) and Feimer, Pommersheim, and Wise (1990) found that in South Dakota sentencing for Indians was similar to non-Indians. And in some cases they found that non-Indians received statistically more severe punishments. Zatz, Lujan & Snyder-Joy (1991) indicate that the inconsistencies within the literature may be attributed to differences between studies of the federal system and studies of state systems. These inconsistencies may also be due the result of variation in use of control variables.

Discrimination against American Indians is reflected in the number of American Indians in the criminal justice system. Peak and Spencer (1987) analyzed data from the Federal Bureau of Investigation (FBI) Uniform Crime Report for 1976 through 1985 comparing American Indians with whites, blacks, and Asians. The researchers found that although Indians represented approximately 0.6 percent of the U.S. population, they accounted for 1.1 percent of all arrests for 1985. Feimer, Pommersheim, and Wise (1990) also document an increase in the number of American Indians being processed through the criminal justice system. Based on data from the Bureau of Justice Statistics, they found that the American Indian prison population increased by 1.2 percent between 1978 and 1984. This rate was double that for whites during the same period.

The dramatic increase in the number of American Indians being processed through the courts and jails could be indicative of discrimination within the criminal justice system. The most effective way to counter negative stereotypes is to educate and demystify the targeted group. Some explanations for discrimination and inequality of American Indians within correctional institutions and courts can be understood by looking at the historical and structural relationship that exists between Indian nations and the U.S. government.

# Government-to-Government Relationship

American Indian nations are unique from other ethnic groups in America because they are not only cultural entities, but, more important, they are political entities. The U. S. government's recognition of Indian nations/tribes as official governments is based on the tribes' sovereign nation status prior to the formation of the U. S. government and is upheld by treaty obligations, international law, and other legally binding agreements. This unique status is commonly referred to as tribal sovereignty.

Although the external sovereignty of tribes has been limited by the U.S. government (e.g., the right to make treaties with other countries), much of the internal sovereignty of tribes remains. Tribal sovereignty is a fundamental concept in understanding American Indian issues. For example, relative to criminal justice, tribal sovereignty adds to the various levels of law to which American Indians are subject, including tribal law, federal law, and state and local law. Jurisdiction is determined by the type of the crime, where the crime occurred, and who was involved.

Deloria and Lytle (1983) contend that American Indian law is one of the most complicated areas of legal study. The jurisdictional problems alone are very complex. The sheer complexity of law and the maintenance of law for American Indians can create confusion and misunderstanding among both the Indian and non-Indian population. In criminal cases, tribal members are subject to at least three levels of government, and criminal jurisdiction is dependent on a number of factors.

Although tribal courts maintain limited jurisdiction in criminal cases, they primarily handle misdemeanor cases involving tribal members (or Indian non-members) that occur on the reservation. Generally, the federal government has the greatest scope of jurisdiction in criminal cases, including all major crimes (e.g., murder, manslaughter, kidnapping, rape, assault with a dangerous weapon, assault resulting in serious bodily injury, arson, burglary, robbery, and other felonies) (Pevar 1992).

The 1990 U.S. census data indicated that half of the individuals who are identified as American Indian live off the reservation in urban or rural areas. Despite this, the majority of American Indians who reside off reservations are closely connected with their reservations and oftentimes live both on and off the reservation. Familiarity with the reservation criminal justice system does not translate to familiarity with the local, state, or federal system.

On many reservations the methods of resolving disputes and crimes are based on traditional concepts of justice. Unlike Euroamerican criminal jurisprudence, which focuses on retribution, the traditional American Indian method of social control primarily emphasizes restitution and compensation. Under Euroamerican notions of criminal jurisprudence, the objectives are to establish fault or guilt and then to punish. The sentencing goals of retribution, revenge, and deterrence and isolation of the offender are extremely important (though the system often pays much lip service to the concept of rehabilitation as well). The idea, therefore, that tribal laws involved some Old Testament eye-for-an-eye mechanism that worked independently of human personality stems merely from inadequate observations of what really occurred in tribal societies. In most instances the system attempted to compensate the victim and his or her family and to solve the problem in such a manner that all could forgive and forget and continue to live within the tribal society in harmony with one another (Deloria & Lytle 1983).

On the other hand, many tribes have been forced to forego traditional methods of tribal government and social control to protect and maintain tribal strength in relation to contemporary American society (Conn 1977). A number of congressional acts have forced tribes to adopt modern political and legal systems. For example, the Indian Reorganization Act of 1934 strongly encouraged tribes to adopt constitutions modeled after the American system of government, regardless of existing tribal government structures. Additionally, the Indian Civil Rights Act of 1968 forced tribes to comply with the general format of American jurisprudence. It imposed the concepts of freedom of religion, speech, press, and assembly on Indians. This created controversy because it undermines tribal sovereignty by placing individual needs over tribal unity.

Tribes have experienced different types of judicial systems over time. Deloria and Lytle (1983) list three types: the traditional court, the Court of Indian Offenses, and tribal court. The primary goal of traditional courts, according to Deloria and Lytle, was to mediate the case to the satisfaction of all involved. The major purpose of traditional courts was to ensure restitution and compensation and to restore harmony within the Indian community. In addition, the composition of traditional courts was not always a body of appointed or elected "judges," rather, offenses were handled by tribal officials, clan members, or family elders. Social control was also enforced through social and religious sanctions, including social ostracism, gossip, and ridicule (Kerr 1969).

Courts of Indian Offenses, also known as Code of Federal Regulation Courts (CFR) because they operate under the written guidelines of the CFR, were established for reservations in the late 1800s by the Department of Interior to intervene in cases involving both whites and Indians (Kerr 1969; Deloria & Lytle 1983). But the courts were also created to assimilate Indians into white society. During the peak of their activity, in the early 1900s, CFR Courts existed on two-thirds of Indian reservations.

The Indian Reorganization Act of 1934 resulted in tribes establishing their own tribal courts and enforcing tribal codes that, although not directly subject to the Department of Interior, were monitored by the Bureau of Indian Affairs (Kerr 1969). Although the Indian Reorganization Act was designed to give authority back to the Indians, many tribes were unable to reinstitute traditional methods of law in the 1930s primarily because the key mechanisms to integrate and uphold a traditional legal system, such as religion, had already been disrupted by assimilation pressures.

# Political, Social, and Demographic Characteristics of Federally Recognized Tribes

There are more than 510 federally recognized tribes in the United States, including approximately 200 tribes in Alaska. Federally recognized means that the tribes have a special, legal relationship with the U.S. government. Two federal agencies are assigned the primary responsibility of the federal government's trust responsibility to tribes: the Bureau of Indian Affairs (BIA) and the Indian Health Service (IHS).

Located within the U.S. Department of Interior, the BIA has the primary responsibility of working with tribes in areas related to land, education, and welfare. The BIA's stated goal is to support tribes by providing technical assistance, as well as programs and services, through twelve area offices and 109 agencies and special offices located across the United States (BIA 1991). The BIA has been severely criticized by the tribes for historically being a paternalistic and inefficient agency. In 1990, under pressure from tribes and Congress, the BIA began efforts to work more closely with tribes through several activities: establishing a tribal advisory committee (National Advisory Task Force), involving tribes in the budgetary process, and emphasizing the government-to-government relationship as mandated by law.

Located within the Department of Health and Human Services, the IHS has a primary responsibility to assist tribes in health-related issues. The IHS comprises twelve area offices and seventy-eight service units that administer forty-three hospitals and 121 health centers (IHS 1991). IHS operates hospitals and clinics on reservations and provides related health services for Indian communities. These federal health services are based on federal laws explicitly specified in the Constitution and in other pertinent authorities (IHS 1991). In addition to these agencies, other federal agencies, including the Departments of Housing and Urban Development, Energy, Education, Agriculture, and Commerce, also work directly with tribes.

Only tribes that are federally recognized have a trust relationship with the federal government. There are a number of tribes and groups in the United States that are not recognized by the federal government. These tribes and groups may or may not have state recognition. Many of these groups are seeking federal recognition. Since 1978, eight tribes out of 126 tribes and groups that have petitioned for recognition have received acknowledgment of tribal status from the BIA, and twelve have been denied. Twelve other groups bypassed the BIA and gained federal recognition through action by Congress (BIA 1991). One of the basic requirements of federal recognition is that the tribe must show evidence that its government and culture have been in continuous existence prior to the establishment of the U.S. government.

Each tribe maintains a list of individuals who are legally enrolled members. Tribal enrollment requirements differ for each tribe. The majority require that members be at least one-forth degree Indian heritage. Recently, there have been a number of non-Indians falsely claiming to be American Indian believing that they may benefit from this declaration. However, verification of an individual's claims of American Indian heritage can be made by asking them for documentation or contacting the tribe directly.

# Diversity of Tribes

Although there are some important similarities among Indian nations, such as the devastating effect of the invasion of Western Europeans and the subsequent repression as reflected in the U.S. government's Indian policies, there are important differences among tribes. Tribes differ in language, population, land base, economy, physical characteristics, and government structure, including the form and content of their tribal codes, laws, and courts. In addition, tribes differ in their social conditions, such as levels of income, education, and employment. Not only are there differences in social and economic status among tribes but there are also differences within tribes among individual members.

According to the 1990 U. S. Census report, there were approximately 2 million people who are self-identified as American Indians, half of whom live off the reservation in urban or rural areas. The U.S. Census reveals that American Indians are one of the fastest-growing populations in the United States today. According to a 1991 IHS report, the birth rate for American Indians and Alaskan Natives residing in thirty-three reservation states was 28.0 (rate per 1,000 population) from 1986 through 1988. This is 13 percent higher than the birthrate for all races are considered in the U.S. In addition, the Indian population is a young population. In 1980, 32 percent of the American Indian population was younger than fifteen years, and 5 percent was older than sixty-four. For all the races in the United States, the corresponding values were 23 percent and 11 percent, respectively (IHS 1991).

The average life expectancy of American Indians has gradually increased. Currently the life expectancy at birth is approximately three years below that of the U.S. white population. The average annual income for Indian families in 1979 was less than $14,000 compared with white families in the United States with an annual income of almost $21,000 (Snipp & Summers 1991).

The education level of American Indians is gradually increasing. In 1970 only 22 percent of American Indians completed high school compared with 55 percent of whites. In 1980 the percentage of American Indians completing high school had increased to 56 percent compared with 69 percent for whites. These gains may be misleading because General Equivalency Diplomas among American Indians are widespread, and in 1980, 26 percent of Indian youths between the ages of 16 and 19 had withdrawn from school without a diploma (Snipp 1992).

Despite these caveats there is a steady number of American Indians entering professional occupations, such as law, medicine, and the social sciences. Many of these individuals are applying their skills to strengthen the position of American Indian tribes.

Tribal governments are more stable than they have been since the mid-1800s when the U.S. government's assimilative policies took a devastating toll on the internal structure and fabric of tribes. Today, there is a renaissance of tribal traditions, language, and religion. Tribal governments are encouraging members to teach and learn their language and to participate in tribal religion and culture. Along with the rejuvenation of tribal governments has come effective efforts toward self-determinating governments. Of late, economic endeavors, such as Indian gaming (gambling), have emphasized the unique status that Indian nations have with the federal government.

Tribunal political unity and activism are on the increase. Tribes are joining together to protect their sovereignty and to assume their position among the balance of powers along with the states and the federal government. This is evident in the unified efforts of tribes in successfully lobbying the U.S. Congress to place a permanent moratorium on a 1990 U.S. Supreme Court decision (*Duro v. Reina* 1990) that would have seriously limited tribal jurisdiction. This unified activism among tribes is also evident in the manner in which, for example, the Arizona tribes have organized against the state's attempt to restrict them from determining the type of economic development they wish to pursue as it relates to the establishment and operation of gambling enterprises.

Stereotypes change depending on the perceptions of the group. The more threatening a group is perceived to be, the more negative the stereotype. If tribal sovereignty and self-determination are viewed as threatening to the surrounding non-Indian community, this could result in more negative stereotyping and greater discrimination directed toward American Indians.

# Conclusion

There are a number of explanations that have been presented regarding the harsh treatment American Indians receive in the criminal justice system (Zatz, Lujan & Snyder-Joy 1991). The two areas that appear to have the most dramatic effect on how American Indians are processed through the criminal justice system include the racist stereotyping and labeling, particularly as it relates to alcohol, and cultural and language factors.

The issue of class is also an important factor that may have a negative compounding influence on stereotyping and treatment of Indians within the criminal justice system. The income for the majority of the American Indian population is far below that of the general U.S. population. It is likely that their lower socioeconomic standing contributes to their discrimination within the criminal justice system.

Age is also an important factor. The majority of crimes are usually committed by young adults, and the American Indian population is a youthful population. The combination of elements such as youth, unemployment, racism, and stereotyping can lead to inequality for American Indians within the criminal justice system.

Cultural and social differences influence how an individual will react and be treated in a particular situation. Tribal courts are more likely to process an individual in a more complete and holistic manner and operate in a less formal manner than non-Indian courts. The primary goal for many tribal courts is to reintegrate the individual back into the community. On the other hand, because of the incredible number of offenders who must be processed through the non-Indian courts, there is an emphasis on efficiency and formality with a concentration on incarceration and punishment. This contradiction in focus and intent of the two systems enhances the complexity of an already difficult situation and increases the likelihood of misinterpretation and stereotyping.

Some possible solutions to the problem of stereotypes would be to increase understanding through readings and direct interaction with American Indians. There are a number of excellent books by American Indian scholars, researchers, and writers that could provide valuable insight on American Indian issues. Efforts should be made to include American Indians in the justice system by recruiting and hiring them and involving them in decision- making aspects of the judicial process. Areas with large American Indian populations should involve American Indians in policy decisions by appointing them to various advisory committees and panels. Non-Indians should not assume that Indian people are guilty or that they understand the process.

American Indians need to familiarize themselves with their rights and the various legal systems with which they may come in contact. A far-reaching program on legal education should be implemented by tribal governments and urban Indian programs. This can be done through various forms of mass media, schools, and special events. For some large Indian reservations, the radio is the most effective form of communication.

# References

Bennion, L., and T. K. Li. 1976. Alcohol metabolism in American Indians and whites. *New England Journal of Medicine* 284:9-13.

Burkey, R. M. 1978. *Ethnic and racial groups: The dynamics of dominance.* Menlo Park, Calif.: Cummings Publishing Co.

Bureau of Indian Affairs. 1991. *American Indians today: Answers to your questions*, 3rd edition. Washington, D.C.: U.S. Department of the Interior.

Bynum, T. S., and R. Paternoster. 1984. Discrimination revisited: An exploration of frontstage and backstage criminal justice decision making. *Sociology and Social Research* 69:90-108.

Conn, S. 1977. Mid-passage—The Navajo tribe and its first legal revolution. *American Indian Law Review* 6 (2):329-70.

Deloria, V., Jr. 1980. The American Indian image in North America. In *The pretend Indians: Images of Native Americans in the movies*, ed. G. M. Bataille and L. P. Silet. Ames, Iowa: Iowa State University Press.

Deloria, V., Jr., and C. M. Lytle. 1983. *American Indians, American justice*. Austin, Texas: University of Texas Press.

Farris, J. J., and B. M. Jones 1978. Ethanol metabolism in male American Indians and whites. *Alcoholism: Clinical and Experimental Research* 2 (1):77-81.

Feimer, S., F. Pommersheim, and S. Wise. 1990. Marking time: Does race make a difference? A study of disparate sentencing in South Dakota. *Journal of Crime and Justice* 13:86-102.

Fenna, D., et al. 1971. Ethanol metabolism in various racial groups. *Canadian Medical Association Journal* 105:472-75.

Freire, P. 1985. *Pedagogy of the oppressed*. New York: Continuum Publishing Corp.

Indian Health Service. 1991. *Trends in Indian health—1991*. Washington, D.C.: U.S. Department of Health and Human Services.

Hall, E. L., and A. Simkus. 1975. Inequality in the types of sentences received by Native Americans and whites. *Criminology* 13 (2):199-122.

Kerr, J. R. 1969. Constitutional rights, tribal justice and the American Indian. *Journal of Public Law* 18:311-38.

Levy, J. E., S. Kunitz, and M. Everett. 1969. Navajo criminal homicide. *Southwestern Journal of Anthropology* 25:124-49.

May, P. A., and M. B. Smith. 1988. Some Navajo Indian opinions about alcohol abuse and prohibition: A survey and recommendations for policy. *Journal of Studies on Alcohol* 49:324-34.

Peak, K., and J. Spencer. 1987. Crime in Indian country: Another "Trail of Tears." *Journal of Criminal Justice* 15:485-94.

Pevar, S. L. 1992. *The rights of Indians in tribes*, 2d edition. An American Civil Liberties Union Handbook. Carbondale: Southern Illinois University Press.

Pommersheim, F., and S. Wise. 1989. Going to the penitentiary. A study of disparate sentencing in South Dakota. *Criminal Justice and Behavior* 16:155-65.

Riffenburgh, A. S. 1964. Cultural influences and crime among Indian-Americans of the Southwest. *Federal Probation* 28 (3):38-46.

Schaefer, J. M. 1981. Firewater myths revisited. *Journal of Studies on Alcohol* 9:99-117.

Snipp, C. M., and G. F. Summers. 1991. American Indians and economic poverty. In *Rural Poverty in America*, ed. C. Duncan. Westport, Conn.: Auburn House.

Snipp, C. M. 1992. Sociological perspectives on American Indians. Annual Review. *Sociology* 18:351-71.

Stewart, O. 1964. Questions regarding Indian criminality. *Human Organization* 23:61-66.

Stratton, J. 1973. Cops and drunks: Police attitudes and actions in dealing with Indian drunks. *The International Journal of Addictions* 8 (4):613-621.

Swift, B., and G. Bickel. 1974. *Comparative parole treatment of American Indians and non-Indians at U.S. federal prisons.* Washington, D.C.: Bureau of Social Science Research.

Weber, S. R. 1982. Native Americans before the bench: The nature of contrast and conflict in Native-American law ways and western legal systems. *The Social Science Journal* 19:47-55.

Wilkinson, G. 1974. Colonialism through the media. *The Indian Historian* 7 (Summer):29-32.

Zatz, M., C. C. Lujan, and Z. Snyder-Joy. 1991. American Indians and criminal justice. In *Race and criminal justice*, ed. by M. Lynch and E. B. Patterson. New York: Harrow and Heston.

Zeiner, A. R., A. Paredes, and L. Cowden. 1976. Physiologic responses to ethanol among the Tarahumara Indians. *Annals of the New York Academy of Sciences* 273:151-58.

# 8. Asian Americans and Pacific Islanders: Minorities Within A Minority

*By Lawrence K. Koseki, D.S.W.*

In any examination of Asian Americans and Pacific Islanders and corrections one faces two dilemmas. The first is the lack of precision and specificity in the definition of Asian Americans and Pacific Islanders. The second is the dearth of information about the nature, extent, and characteristics of Asian Americans and Pacific Islanders in general and offenders in correctional settings in particular. This chapter will endeavor to sharpen the definition of Asian Americans/Pacific Islanders, provide a brief sociodemographic profile of this diverse population, offer several cultural aspects and dimensions relating to Asian Americans/Pacific Islanders, and propose an intercultural corrections approach that can increase ethnic and cultural awareness of Asian Americans/Pacific Islanders.

## Historical Roots

According to the U.S. Census Bureau, the term "Asian Americans/Pacific Islanders" refers to a set of U.S. population subgroups with roots in countries of origins in the Far East, Southeast Asia, and the Pacific Islands (American Public Health Association 1982). Also included are people from the Indian subcontinent (O'Hare 1992). As the term suggests, the classification consists of two major population subgroups. The Asian American subgroup includes peoples whose ancestral origins are from Bangladesh, Bhutan, Burma, Cambodia, China, Taiwan, Mongolia, Japan, Korea,

*Lawrence K. Koseki, D.S.W., is an Associate Professor of Public Health at the University of Hawaii at Manoa, Honolulu.*

Hong Kong, Macau, Malaysia, Indonesia, Maldives, Nepal, Pakistan, India, Singapore, Sri Lanka, Laos, Thailand, Vietnam, and the Philippines. The Pacific Islander subgroup is represented by the peoples of Fiji, Guam, Hawaii, Samoa, Tonga, and Micronesia (O'Hare & Felt 1991; Wykle & Kaskel 1991), the latter from such island nations as the Commonwealth of the Northern Marianas, Marshall Islands, Palau, and the Federated States of Micronesia. Although native Hawaiians may be classified as Pacific Islanders by the U.S. Census Bureau, they are also recognized by the federal government as Native Americans under the Older Americans Act, Title VI-B, grants for Native Hawaiian Program (1989) and the federal Native Hawaiian Health Care Act (Public Law 100-579).

There are more than thirty distinct ethnic groups that comprise the Asian American/Pacific Islander census category. Such a classification is essentially a sociopolitical category because these ethnic groups do not share a common language, religion, or culture. This classification was, in part, conceived in the late 1960s and early 1970s as a census-type definition to accommodate the demands from Asian and Pacific Island communities. Because of their small numbers, various Asian and Pacific Island groups realized the need to coalesce to draw the attention of government and nongovernment organizations to their problems and needs. This was especially critical because Asian Americans/Pacific Islanders were keenly aware of society's misconception and pervasive stereotypes of Asian and Pacific Americans being model citizens who took care of their own problems (Koseki 1976).

Asians have a long history in the United States. The Chinese immigrated to America as early as the 1820s (Tseng & Char 1974) and possibly earlier (Miller 1969). Japanese and Filipinos were other major waves of immigration from the Asia-Pacific Basin in the late 1800s and early 1900s. As a result, these groups are represented by sixth and seventh generation Americans as well as recent immigrants with discernible social and cultural differences. In contrast, common among these early immigrants were the prejudice, injustices, and racism they all experienced. Another common characteristic was that they all represented cheap labor imported to do the kinds of work considered unfit for whites (Jacobs & Landau 1971).

Recent immigrants, especially those from Southeast Asian countries, face problems similar to those earlier immigrants—that of low English literacy, low socioeconomic status, difficulties in adapting to the customs and mores of their newly adopted country, and the racism and discrimination that all minority groups experience.

Before the term "Asian American/Pacific Islander" became institutionalized, various Asian and Pacific Island groups relied on ethnic-specific, American labels (e.g., Chinese-American, Japanese-American, Korean-American, and Filipino-American). Such labels sent a message to the majority society that they too were American citizens, despite their different physical characteristics and the fact that many of their parents were non-English-speaking aliens without rights of citizenship. For Japanese-Americans, being a hyphenated American took on greater meaning at the outbreak of World War II with serious challenges to their patriotism and loyalty and by the mass evacuation of Japanese-Americans to concentration camps without due process (Thomas & Nishimoto 1969; Weglyn 1976).

Asian Americans and Pacific Islanders are less homogeneous than they first appear because of ethnic-specific groups and cohort and generational differences. This population represents the most diverse of America's major minority groups, and considering the continuing pervasive stereotypes, perceptions, and beliefs in our society, a study of Asian Americans/Pacific Islanders should be approached with care.

# Sociodemographic Characteristics

The most significant demographic factor about the Asian American/Pacific Islander group is its phenomenal growth rate over the past two decades. It is currently the fastest growing group in the Unite States. Between 1980 and 1990, the growth rate of Asian Americans/Pacific Islanders was nearly 108 percent compared with about 9 percent for the overall U.S. population (Chen 1993). In 1980, the Asian American/Pacific Islander population was estimated to be 3.8 million. (See Table 1.) By 1989, triggered by an immigration of more than 2.8 million people (see Table 2), the Asian American/Pacific Islander group increased to an estimated 6.9 million or 2.8 percent of the total U.S. population (O'Hare & Felt 1991).

The rapid increase of the Asian American/Pacific Islander population began in the 1960s and grew a phenomenal 141 percent

74

**Table 1**

**Asians and Pacific Islanders in the United States by Country of Origin, 1980**

| Country of Origin | Population 1980 | |
|---|---|---|
| | *Number* | *Percent* |
| China* | 812,178 | 22 |
| Philippines | 781,894 | 21 |
| Japan | 716,331 | 19 |
| India | 387,223 | 10 |
| Korea | 357,393 | 10 |
| Vietnam | 245,025 | 7 |
| Samoa/Tonga/Guam | 76,441 | 2 |
| Laos** | 52,887 | 1 |
| Thailand | 45,279 | 1 |
| Cambodia | 16,044 | —† |
| Pakistan | 15,792 | —† |
| Other | 219,953 | 6 |
| **TOTAL** | **3,726,440** | **100** |

*\* Includes Taiwan, Hong Kong, and Macau.*
*\*\*Includes Hmong.*
*†Represents less than 0.5 percent.*
*Source:* Subject reports, Asian and Pacific Islander Population in the United States: 1980. *Bureau of the Census. PC 80-2-1E. Washington, D.C.: GPO 1983.*

during the 1970s. Significant numbers of immigrants from Asia-Pacific countries contributed to the surge of population growth in the 1980s in which three-fourths of the increase was due to immigration (O'Hare & Felt 1991).

In the 1980s, two immigration waves were identified. One was from Asian countries (China, Korea, and the Philippines) with fairly large numbers already living in the United States. For them, immigration meant family reunification and establishment of kinship

| Table 2 | | |
|---|---|---|
| **Asian and Pacific Islander Immigrants and Refugees by Country of Origin, 1980-89** | | |
| **Country of Origin** | **Immigration/Refugee 1980-89** | |
| | *Number* | *Percent* |
| China* | 443,031 | 15 |
| Philippines | 473,831 | 17 |
| Japan | 41,739 | 1 |
| India | 253,781 | 9 |
| Korea | 338,891 | 12 |
| Vietnam | 679,378 | 24 |
| Samoa/Tonga/Guam | 6,214 | —† |
| Laos** | 256,727 | 9 |
| Thailand | 59,638 | 2 |
| Cambodia | 210,724 | 7 |
| Pakistan | 55,900 | 2 |
| Other | 55,485 | 2 |
| **TOTAL** | **2,865,339** | **100** |

*Includes Taiwan, Hong Kong, and Macau.*
**Includes Hmong.*
† *Represents less than 0.5 percent.*
*Source:* 1989 statistical yearbook. *Immigration and Naturalization Service. Washington, D.C.: GPO, 1990.*

ties for those who were highly educated to meet employment requirements under immigration laws. The second wave, which was facilitated by U.S. policies following the end of the Vietnam War, included immigrants and refugees from war-torn Southeast Asian countries such as Vietnam, Laos, and Cambodia (O'Hare & Felt 1991). One of the most significant immigration characteristics was the increase in the number of Vietnamese from 245,025 (7 percent) in 1980 to 924,403 (14 percent) in 1989. They have become the third largest subgroup of the Asian American/Pacific Islander group, surpassing those immigrants from Japan, India, and Korea. (See Table 3.) In addition, Laotians and Cambodians registered significant population gains from 1980 to 1989, outpacing Pacific Islanders (Samoans, Tongans, and Guamanians) and Thais. (See Tables 1 and 3.)

| Table 3<br><br>Asians and Pacific Islanders (1980) by Country of Origin<br>Including Immigrants and Refugees (1980-89)<br>in the United States | | |
|---|---|---|
| **Country of Origin** | *Number* | *Percent* |
| China* | 1,245,209 | 18.9 |
| Philippines | 1,255,725 | 19.0 |
| Japan | 758,070 | 11.5 |
| India | 641,004 | 9.7 |
| Korea | 696,284 | 10.6 |
| Vietnam | 924,403 | 14.0 |
| Samoa/Tonga/Guam | 82,655 | 1.3 |
| Laos** | 309,614 | 4.7 |
| Thailand | 104,917 | 1.6 |
| Cambodia | 226,768 | 3.4 |
| Pakistan | 71,692 | 1.1 |
| Other | 275,438 | 4.2 |
| | | |
| **TOTAL** | **6,591,779** | **100** |

*Includes Taiwan, Hong Kong, and Macau.*
**Includes Hmong.*
*Sources:* Subject reports, Asian and Pacific Islander population in the United States: *1980, Bureau of the Census. PC 80-2-1E. Washington, D.C.: GPO, 1983.*
1989 statistical yearbook. *Immigration and Naturalization Service. Washington, D.C.: GPO, 1990.*

The extraordinary growth of Asian Americans/Pacific Islanders in the United States should continue into the 1990s with new immigration quota authorized in 1990 and the preference by American businesses for immigrants with particular work skills and habits (O'Hare & Felt 1991).

## Geographical Distribution

In 1990, 58 percent of all Asian Americans/Pacific Islanders lived in the western region of the United States. More than two-thirds reside in California, Hawaii, New York, Illinois, and New Jersey. California had the largest proportion of Asian Americans/Pacific Islanders, with 40 percent, followed by Hawaii, with 11 percent (O'Hare & Felt 1991). However, Hawaii's Asian Americans/Pacific Islanders represented almost 62 percent of its population while California's Asian Americans/Pacific Islanders comprised slightly less than 10 percent (Chen 1993).

## Education and Income

The Asian Americans/Pacific Islanders have an overall high educational level, although the 1990 Census Population Survey shows that 20 percent of Asian Americans/Pacific Islanders age twenty-five years and over do not have high school diplomas. In comparing economic returns on educational investments, Asian Americans/Pacific Islanders, despite having completed more years of schooling than whites, earned about 21 percent less than whites. This may reflect continuing discrimination against Asian American/Pacific Islander workers (O'Hare & Felt 1991).

The heterogeneity of Asian Americans/Pacific Islanders is also reflected in the range of annual income—the highest wages are earned by Japanese workers, the lowest by Laotians. Compared with the overall poverty level of the U.S. population (12.4 percent), the proportion of poverty among Samoans, Vietnamese, Cambodians, and Laotians ranged from 26 percent, 34 percent, 49 percent, and 66 percent, respectively (Chen 1993). Poverty within Asian American/Pacific Islander communities tends to be shawdowed by the high incomes of a few Asian American/Pacific Islander groups (O'Hare & Felt 1991). In general, the high family income of Asian Americans and Pacific Islanders may be attributed to the following:

- relatively large families
- high number of workers within the family
- tendency to have extended family households
- likelihood of children living at home
- postponement of marriage and childbearing

## *Occupation and Employment*

Although the distribution of Asian Americans and Pacific Islanders by occupation follows a similar pattern as for whites, Asian Americans/Pacific Islanders are more likely to work in manufacturing and trade and in managerial and professional positions and less likely to be in mining, construction, fishing, and farm work.

In 1990, 59 percent of Asian American/Pacific Islander families (compared with 50 percent for whites) received public assistance in the form of cash, Medicaid, food stamps, or low-income energy assistance (O'Hare & Felt 1991). Despite their being stereotyped as shopkeepers and small business operators, Asian Americans/Pacific Islanders are less likely than whites to own small businesses (55 per 1,000 Asian Americans/Pacific Islanders v. 76 per 1,000 whites). These data need to be reviewed within the context that 59 percent of the total Asian American/Pacific Islander population in 1980 was foreign-born (O'Hare & Felt 1991) and were more likely to speak a language other than English in their homes (Chen 1993).

Participation rates for Asian Americans/Pacific Islanders in the labor force show similar overall patterns when compared with whites. However, young adult Asian Americans/Pacific Islanders were more likely to be in school. Older Asian Americans/Pacific Islanders tend to retire later than their white counterparts. This may be the result of cultural work ethics and/or economic necessity (O'Hare & Felt 1991).

Unemployment rates are about the same for Asian Americans/Pacific Islanders and whites. In 1990, the Asian American/Pacific Islander rate was slightly lower (3.5 percent) than for whites (4.2 percent). This low unemployment rate for Asian Americans/Pacific Islanders may be attributed to their high educational attainment and their concentration in large metropolitan areas where more jobs are available (O'Hare & Felt 1991).

## Interracial Marriage and Segregation

Two variables reflect the assimilation and acculturation process for minority groups and newcomers. One is the extent Asian Americans and Pacific Islanders marry people outside their own race. In 1990, 17 percent of Asian Americans/Pacific Islanders reported being married to people of other races. This proportion is about the same for Latinos, but quite higher than the 3 percent for African Americans. The second variable deals with residential segregation. Based on 1980 figures, Asian Americans/Pacific Islanders tended to experience much less residential segregation than African Americans and slightly less segregation than Latinos (O'Hare & Felt 1991).

# Cultural Aspects

The word "culture" is possibly one of the most complex constructs in American society. At a nominal level, it can be defined as the total, integrated pattern of human behavior that includes thought, speech, and action that is learned and perpetuated by succeeding generations. According to Webster's, culture can also be defined as a set of customs, beliefs, social forms, and material traits of a racial, religious, or social group. Ethnicity, on the other hand, relates to physical and mental traits possessed by the members of a group as a product of their common heredity and cultural traditions or ties (racial, linguistic, and cultural) with a specific group.

An ethnic group can also represent a self-perceived group of people who share a past but may also not fit the types of census definitions bureaucratically conceived. Furthermore, classification based on ancestral descent may or may not be self-perceived (Maretzki 1974). These concepts and definitions are important to understanding and appreciating the vast differences of the more than thirty population subgroups that fall under the Asian American/Pacific Islander umbrella.

Although culture also represents a way of life, it is important to be aware that the analytic value is applicable to groups and not to individuals. In other words, knowledge of culture does not necessarily reveal much about an individual and his or her behavior. A common error is to equate group membership and its presumed cultural characteristics with individual behavior.

Cultural aspects are important variables in assessing the operation of culture because they may explain a significant part of the inmate behavior. They lead to understanding how values and cultural beliefs may affect an individual's behavior and attitudes, especially in interaction with others in a confined setting. But cultural and ethnic backgrounds alone are not in themselves sufficient guides for corrections staff because different cultures have different views of what constitutes right and wrong behavior (Maretzki 1974).

Although it is not feasible to launch a more in-depth analysis of the differences among the various Asian American/Pacific Islander groups in this chapter, several cultural dimensions and factors are offered as an initial guide to increase cultural awareness of Asian Americans/Pacific Islanders as a very diverse and heterogeneous group (Warren & Palafox 1985):

1. The term "Asian Americans/Pacific Islanders" is not a cultural or ethnic classification that is useful in understanding the cultural influences on an individual's behavior or lifestyle. One important aspect, then, is to determine the ethnic-specific group with which an individual identifies.

2. Many Asian Americans/Pacific Islanders are multi-generations in the United States and differ significantly in their acculturation and adaptation to American lifestyle. Many others, however, are foreign-born and speak little or no English.

3. Within each distinct ethnic group, a discernible region of origin can be differentiated. For example, there are regional differences between Japanese and Okinawans and between Japanese of various prefectures from the main islands of Japan; for Filipinos, differences are evident by ethnic subgroupings and dialects, such as Ilocano, Visayan, and Tagalog; for Vietnamese, there are differences according to whether one is Vietnamese or Vietnamese of Chinese origin.

# Asian Americans and Pacific Islanders and Corrections

A literature search on Asian Americans/Pacific Islanders in correctional facilities reveals a dearth of information about the nature, extent, and characteristics of the incarcerated segment of this population. Consultations with ethnic studies scholars, criminal justice academicians, and corrections officials confirm the paucity of investigations and research of Asian American/Pacific Islander offenders in correctional settings.

This lack of information may be the result of the statistical invisibility of Asian Americans/Pacific Islanders in the United States in general and in correctional facilities in particular. It may be because of the way information and statistics are collected and maintained (e.g., subsuming Asian Americans/Pacific Islanders under the category of "Other"). It may also be that the number of Asian Americans/Pacific Islanders in prison is in fact very small and therefore has not attracted the attention of criminologists, researchers, and social scientists. However, if the Asian American/Pacific Islander population continues its phenomenal growth, the acculturation process for Asian American/Pacific Islander immigrants and the newly arrived may lead to more intercultural conflicts that can result in a rise in crime and delinquency (Kitano 1969).

The lack of any baseline information about Asian Americans/Pacific Islanders in prison begs for the simplest exploratory and descriptive studies. A dire need exists to support research that includes even nonrepresentative Asian American/Pacific Islander offender samples so that an Asian American/Pacific Islander corrections database can be developed to increase understanding of the breadth and diversity within and across the subpopulation groups comprising this category.

Hawaii, according to its corrections officials, is one of the few states that collects inmate population data by ethnic-specific categories. (See Table 4.) The distribution of inmate population by ethnicity can be compared with the state or county population to assess each group's proportional relation to the general population. As Table 4 indicates, all Asian Americans/Pacific Islanders, with the exception of native Hawaiians, were underrepresented in the inmate population across the state. Native Hawaiians were the largest single

**Table 4**

**Distribution of Hawaii State Population and Statewide Inmate Census by Ethnicity**

| Ethnicity | State Population* | | Inmate Population** | |
|---|---|---|---|---|
| | *Number* | *Percent* | *Number* | *Percent* |
| Black | 20,656 | 2.0 | 145 | 5.3 |
| Caucasian | 250,102 | 24.0 | 627 | 22.9 |
| Chinese | 50,138 | 4.8 | 25 | 0.9 |
| Filipino | 117,471 | 11.3 | 216 | 7.9 |
| Japanese | 241,637 | 23.1 | 93 | 3.4 |
| Korean | 11,892 | 1.1 | 25 | 0.9 |
| Native Hawaiian | 210,738 | 20.2 | 959 | 35.0 |
| Samoan | 6,249 | 0.6 | 107 | 3.9 |
| Mixed | 119,301 | 11.4 | — | — |
| Other/Unknown | 15,847 | 1.5 | 542† | 19.8 |
| | | | | |
| TOTALS | 1,044,031 | 100 | 2,739 | 100 |

*Source: Table 23, State of Hawaii data book: A statistical abstract, 1990.
**Source: Corrections information system and Public Safety Department weekly population reports, fiscal year 1992, Hawaii State Department of Public Safety.
†Includes persons of mixed ancestry, Hispanics, and other smaller Asian/Pacific groups.

ethnic group in prison, almost double their proportion of the general population.

Fifteen years ago, native Hawaiian inmates comprised nearly 47 percent of the state's inmate population, while representing only about 12 percent in the general population. During this period, blacks were also slightly overrepresented. All Asian Americans/Pacific Islanders and whites were underrepresented in the state's inmate population (Koseki 1978). Since 1978, the following trends can be noted: Native Hawaiians, despite a significant decrease in 1992, continue to be the single largest ethnic inmate population group. Caucasian and black inmates have almost doubled their proportions in prison. Chinese, Japanese, Koreans, and Filipinos continue to reflect decreasing proportions in the state prison population.

In spite of Hawaii's rich multiethnic population and its culturally diverse prison population, little research has been conducted on cultural factors and their relationship to behavioral manifestations of inmates. Over 50 percent of all marriages in Hawaii now involve individuals of different ethnic backgrounds. This racial and cultural mingling has resulted in an intercultural identity for many individuals (Warren & Palafox 1980), including those in correctional facilities. Such intercultural identities unique to Hawaii's predominantly Asian and Pacific Islander population present challenges in operationalizing the terms "culture" and "ethnicity" and can complicate comparisons with Asian Americans/Pacific Islanders elsewhere.

The underrepresentation of Hawaii's Asian Americans/Pacific Islanders in prison (with the exception of native Hawaiians) may reflect a similar situation for Asian Americans/Pacific Islanders in correctional facilities nationwide. If accurate, such an underrepresentation, especially in states with heavy concentrations of Asian Americans/Pacific Islanders could lead to their further invisibility and minimization of the problems Asian Americans/Pacific Islanders face in or out of prison.

# Implications

The current lack of information on Asian Americans/Pacific Islanders in prison may well be that they are underrepresented relative to their numbers in the general population. Yet, Asian Americans/Pacific Islanders and the other major minority groups now accounting for 25 percent of the U.S. population are expected to grow to 47 percent by the year 2050. These percentages will be affected by continuing high rates of immigration, a younger age structure, and higher fertility among some of these groups. The minority populations in the United States, as a result, will also become much more diverse (O'Hare 1992). Thus, society and its institutions will need to be aware of the increasing diversity of

Americans who represent multi-intercultural identities, which, at the minimum, will require redefinitions of culture and ethnicity. These significant demographic trends in the U.S. population should also signal the need for new approaches in corrections for the twenty-first century.

Intercultural corrections is premised on the assumption that inmates and correctional officers, in most cases, represent different cultural backgrounds and that such differences can lead to a host of problems ranging from miscommunication, both verbal and nonverbal, to differences in beliefs and perceptions based on one's personal experience, family and social situation, and environment. Individuals in authority can encounter difficulties without an appreciation of cultural differences in attitudes toward and in relation to authority. Difficulties are compounded when correctional staff tend to interpret behavior or other manifestations only from their own cultural perspective without realizing that there may be other meanings and interpretations. Even when inmates and correctional officers have similar ethnic and cultural backgrounds, the intercultural corrections model calls for continuous questioning of what is normal and appropriate within a cultural context.

The intercultural corrections approach can be useful in enhancing understanding of Asian American/Pacific Islander offenders when the following cultural factors and ethnic dimensions are examined and ascertained:

- ethnic-specific group identification of the offender either through self-declaration/perception or by familial confirmation
- ethnic subgroupings of particular ethnic groups (i.e., Ilocano, Tagalog, or Visayan of the Filipinos) with language as well as distinct geocultural differences
- country and region of origin
- country of birth, (e.g., United States or foreign-born)
- generations or length of time in the United States
- level of English literacy
- membership in ethnic-social and religious organizations

When confronted with behavior that may be culturally rooted, correctional officials should consult with appropriate ethnic representatives from the community to help with such matters as language translation, cultural meanings and interpretations, and social support for the inmate. Most ethnic groups, especially recent immigrants from Southeast Asia, generally have organized mutual assistance associations that can be used as resources.

Correctional facilities and institutions can become more culturally sensitive by examining their ethnic composition of the workforce and the inmate population. If large ethnic disparities exist, it behooves correctional employers to recruit and hire underrepresented groups to narrow such gaps. The responsibility rests with the correctional institution to seek and promote equal treatment in employment and access to services for those of all cultures (Koseki 1980).

Racial differences per se are minimally important in dividing people or in creating conflict. More important are those situations or relationships in which attitudes and behavior come to play between groups. Even an encyclopedic knowledge of race and racial differences will throw little light on solving problems when certain groups are on unequal terms (McWilliams 1964).

Although cultural insights can be heightened by increasing one's understanding and appreciation of the broad spectrum of groups and subgroups comprising the Asian American and Pacific Islander category, the proverbial bottom line for all correctional staff in dealing effectively with Asian Americans and Pacific Islanders and other ethnic minorities is firm and fair treatment of all inmates—a philosophy and practice that incorporate honesty, authenticity, and treating inmates as human beings.

# References

American Public Health Association. 1982. *Health of minorities and women: Chartbook.* Washington, D.C.: American Public Health Association.

Chen, Jr., M. S. 1993. Cardiovascular health among Asian Americans/Pacific Islanders: An examination of health status and intervention approaches. *American Journal of Health Promotion* 7 (January/February): 199-207.

Jacobs, P., and S. Landau. 1971. *To serve the devil Colonials and sojourners.* New York: Random House.

Kitano, Harry H. L. 1969. *Japanese Americans.* Englewood Cliffs, N.J.: Prentice-Hall.

Koseki, L. K. 1976. *Asian American social workers: A case study of organizational development.* Unpublished doctoral dissertation, University of Southern California, Los Angeles.

Koseki, L. K. 1978. *Capital punishment in Hawaii: An ethnic perspective.* Chicago: Asian American Mental Health Research Center.

Koseki, L. K. 1980. Affirmative action in corrections: Issues, dilemmas, and alternatives. *Corrections Today* 42 (November/December): 84-87, 92.

Maretzki, T. W. 1974. Culture and the individual. In *People and cultures in Hawaii*, ed. W. S. Tseng, J. F. McDermott, Jr., and T. W. Maretzki, 1-7. Honolulu: University of Hawaii School of Medicine.

McWilliams, C. 1964. *Brothers under the skin.* Boston: Little, Brown and Company.

Miller, S. C. 1969. *The unwelcome immigrant: The American image of the Chinese*, 1785-1882. Berkeley, Calif.: The University of California Press.

O'Hare, W. P. 1992. America's minorities: The demographics of diversity. *Population Bulletin* 47 (December).

O'Hare, W. P., and J. C. Felt. 1991. *Asian Americans: America's fastest growing minority group.* Washington, D.C.: Population Reference Bureau.

Thomas, D. S., and R. Nishimoto. 1969. *The spoilage: Japanese-American evacuation and resettlement during World War II.* Berkeley, Calif.: University of California Press.

Tseng, W. S., and W. F. Char. 1974. The Chinese in Hawaii. In *People and cultures in Hawaii*, ed. W. S. Tseng, J. F. McDermott, Jr., and T. W. Maretzki, 24-33. Honolulu: University of Hawaii School of Medicine.

Warren, A., and N. Palafox. 1985. Introduction. In *Cross-cultural caring*, 2d ed., ed. N. Palafox and A. Warren, 1-7. Honolulu: John A. Burns School of Medicine, University of Hawaii.

Weglyn, M. 1976. *Years of infamy: The untold story of America's concentration camps*. New York: William Morrow and Company.

Wykle, M., and B. Kaskel. 1991. Increasing the longevity of minority older adults through improved health status. In *Minority elders: Longevity, economics, and health*, 24-31. Washington, D.C.: Gerontological Society of America.

# 9. Diversity in the Workplace

*By Theodore H. Curry II, Ph.D.*

**A**s the U.S. population changes, so does its workforce. The population is aging because of improved health care and the deluge of baby boomers born between 1946 and 1964. The passage of the Americans with Disabilities Act in 1990 drew attention to the needs of the disabled population. The number of individuals with disabilities in the workforce is expected to increase.

America is now, and has been since its inception, the destination of choice for immigrants. Two-thirds of all global migration is into the United States. In 1908, playwright Israel Zangwill made the now famous statement: "America. It's God's crucible; the great melting pot where all the races of Europe are melting and reforming"(Copeland 1988). At that time, European newcomers were eager to shed their own culture and heritages and become homogenized Americans. That is not, however, the immigrant picture today. Most of the immigrants to the United States are from contrasting cultures that do not blend readily into American life.

This chapter will discuss (1) changes in the U.S. labor force that are occurring and that are projected to occur, (2) implications of these changes, (3) why the resulting diversity must be encouraged, planned for, and accepted, and (4) actions corrections professionals should take to deal effectively with co-workers from diverse cultures.

---

*Theodore H. Curry II, Ph.D., is associate director and professor of the graduate School of Labor and Industrial Relations at Michigan State University.*

# The Changing Labor Force and Its Implications

## *An Aging Labor Force*

The U.S. workforce is aging for three primary reasons. First, an increased life expectancy from improved health care has allowed Americans to live longer and, hence, to work longer. Second, most laws requiring retirement because of age have been removed. Concerns about their retirement incomes lead many workers to choose to work until an older age. Third, the large number of babies born between 1946 and 1964, the so-called baby boomers, is moving through the population, increasing the median age. That phenomenon has resulted in the following:

1. In 1987 the median age of the workforce was thirty-six. By the year 2000 the median age is expected to rise to thirty-nine.

2. The share of the workforce between the ages of thirty-five and fifty-four is increasing.

3. The share of workers between the ages of fifty-five and sixty-four will be declining through the mid-1990s, but will begin to rise when the baby boomers reach this age level.

4. The share of the workforce between the ages of sixteen and thirty-four is declining.

The implications of this aging labor force are many and profound. The already burdened health care system will continue to be taxed by an older labor force that demands more health care. In fact, many employers are beginning to grapple not only with child care issues but with the parental care responsibilities that many of their employees now face and will continue to face.

This large pool of older workers in the labor force, coupled with a flattening of organizational hierarchies, causes the phenomenon known as career plateauing, where opportunities to rise to the top of organizations are limited. On the positive side, the large numbers of older workers may create a profusion of employees interested in part-time employment. Part-time employment is a major trend in the United States as employers attempt to match their human resource needs with their work demands.

## More Women

During the past few decades the increased number of women working outside the home has dramatically added to the diversity of the U.S. workforce. In 1960 an estimated 19 percent of women with children were in the workforce. By 1984 that number had risen to 61 percent and in 1992 may exceed 70 percent. Add to this a boom of single-parent families—most headed by women—and it is clear that the large numbers of women in the workforce is a phenomenon that is here to stay. In fact, an estimated 64 percent of workforce growth during the 1990s will be accounted for by women (Johnston & Packer 1987).

The increased number of women working in correctional agencies that resulted from pressures brought by equal employment opportunity and affirmative action challenges and initiatives will continue. In addition, the push for employer-sponsored or -supported child care, flexible benefits, and flexible work hours is likely to continue. As with older workers, more women in the labor force may also lead to more part-time workers.

## More Minorities

Multiculturalism in the U.S. workforce is most noteworthy when it comes to minorities. Ethnicity in the workplace is increasing and intensifying as new immigrants, predominantly from Asia and Latin America, find it difficult to blend into the mainstream. As a result, many Americans must interact with people who are culturally different from themselves. By the year 2000, the African-American workforce will increase by an estimated 29 percent, the Hispanic workforce by 74 percent, and other races by 70 percent. According to Johnston and Packer (1987), by the year 2000, 85 percent of the growth in the U.S. workforce will be represented by women and minorities. Demographers estimate that if birth rates and immigration patterns continue, those Americans who are now thought of as minorities will be the majority by 2030 (Johnston & Packer 1987).

Managing and working in a culturally diverse workplace will be the norm for more and more U.S. workers. The implications are tremendous. Employees will face differences in verbal and nonverbal communication. Values that may lead to different ways of doing things and different dietary and grooming habits must be understood and accepted.

## Workers with Disabilities

Another component of the diverse workforce is the increased number of workers with disabilities. The 1990 Americans with Disabilities Act prohibits employment discrimination against individuals with disabilities in the public- and private-sector workforce by employers of fifteen or more employees.

This law removes employment barriers for the more than 34 million Americans with disabilities, allowing more of these individuals to enter the workforce. The law means that jobs and procedures will need to be redesigned, nondisabled workers will need to be trained to be more comfortable with colleagues with disabilities, and alternatives, such as home-based employment and telecommuting, will need to be explored.

# Encouraging Diversity

Federal law, through Title VII of the Civil Rights Act of 1964 as amended, the Age Discrimination in Employment Act, and the Americans with Disabilities Act and similar state and local equal employment opportunity statutes, makes race, sex, national origin, age, religion, and disability-based discrimination in the workplace illegal. The legal penalties for noncompliance are serious and have increased with the Civil Rights Act of 1991. In addition, many correctional agencies' employment processes have been subject to scrutiny by federal courts and judges because of violations of the statutes.

Aside from these legal ramifications, many employers are concluding that there are more significant, long-term reasons for encouraging diversity in the workplace. Statistics indicate that as the number of women and minorities in the workplace increases, there will be fewer white men in the workforce. According to Johnston and Packer (1987), only 15 percent of those entering the workforce by the year 2000 will be white men. Employers, including correctional agencies, who choose to limit their labor market to white males will find themselves competing for a decreasing number of workers. Johnston and Packer also predict a shortage of people with skills necessary in a high-tech work environment. Thus, employers will also be competing for skilled employees. Historically, when supply is low and demand is high, prices increase. Therefore, it is costly for employers to fail to value and encourage diversity. Employers who expand their recruitment and selection nets to include men and women from all ages and ethnic groups will be at a competitive advantage.

In the private sector, employers increasingly recognize that, in the global marketplace, a diverse workforce can provide a competitive edge. The U.S. workforce, with all its heterogeneity, provides a boon of potential employees who know the language, culture, and values of a country in which an employer might want to do business. Furthermore, diversity provides a richness of ideas and variety of views—a fertile growing medium for creativity. In correctional agencies, similar benefits can be achieved. The inmate population is multicultural. If the correctional workforce does not reflect that diversity, it will have difficulty communicating, relating, assessing values, and predicting behavior.

# Using Hiring and Training to Encourage Diversity

Managing diversity is defined as "fostering an environment in which workers of all kinds—men, women, white, Hispanic, Asian, Native American, African American, disabled, and elderly—can flourish and, given opportunities to reach their full potential and to contribute at the highest level, can provide an employer top performance" (United States Chamber of Commerce 1992). Before such an environment can be fostered, correctional agencies must make a concerted effort to institute equal employment opportunities and affirmative action in the hiring process. The following suggestions should be considered:

1. Discrimination can be eliminated by ensuring that all

selection devices are job-related (valid), based on a thorough job analysis, and free of cultural bias.

2. Aggressive recruiting from groups that are under-represented must be instituted.

3. All managers involved in the hiring process must be trained and sensitized as to the need for diversity, cultural differences, interviewing do's and don'ts, and fair and consistent assessment of candidates against requirements determined from the job analysis. Managers and human resource specialists need to be thoroughly trained in understanding cultural differences.

4. Realistic goals (not rigid quotas) must be established so that an agency can assess its progress in the hiring and promotion processes. These goals should be set based on the number of people with the requisite skills in a reasonable recruiting area. Managers should be able to show that a good faith effort was made to meet these goals. Similarly, in the promotion process, every correctional agency's leadership team should reflect the diversity of the internal labor force and the external labor market.

Diversity in hiring that is not coupled with training for all and a long-term commitment to managing diversity from top management is doomed. Training should include the following:

1. Organizations and their members, individually and collectively, must be able to discuss issues related to ethnic, racial, cultural, or gender differences in an honest and upfront manner, while protecting each person's sensitivities and not invading his or her private life.

2. General characteristics in values and communication methods of each major minority group (e.g., racial minorities, women, and the disabled) in the workforce should be explored. This exploration should be based on the premise that no one style or pattern is right or better—just different.

3. The unwritten rules of the organization should be explained. All organizations, correctional agencies in-

cluded, have organizational norms and methods that are "understood," but not written. Training around these issues must be specific, especially for employees from outside the mainstream, about rules concerning such things as acceptable language, upward communications, and handling disagreements.

4. Rules regarding antidiscrimination and harassment need to be established or reiterated. Employees must adhere to Equal Employment Opportunity laws and regulations. Agency work rules and practices and grievance and complaint procedures must be highlighted as they pertain to and support affirmative action and workforce diversity.

5. A mentoring program should be developed. Such a program can help to indoctrinate and prepare participants for organizational success.

Training should not be viewed as a one-time thing. It must be an ongoing agency commitment. Managing diversity, understanding cultural differences, and problem solving in a diverse workforce must be on the agenda at staff meetings as well as included in formal training.

Top management commitment is mandatory for handling diversity successfully. Diversity means major changes in organizational values and methods. Such changes are not without controversy, impediments, and setbacks. Top management of a correctional agency must be committed to achieving and managing diversity over the long run so these temporary roadblocks do not become insurmountable. The explicit and implicit signals sent by top management—through its support of diversity in leadership, commitment of agency resources to diversity, attendance at training programs, promotion of high-visibility diversity projects, and swift and forceful responses to people and practices that stand in the path of accomplishing true multiculturalism in the workplace—will determine whether diversity efforts are successful.

# References

Copeland, Lennie. 1988. Valuing diversity, part I: Making the most of cultural differences at the workplace. *Personnel 65* (June):52.

Johnston, W. B., and A. E. Packer. 1987. *Workforce 2000: Work and workers for the 21st century*. Indianapolis: The Hudson Institute.

United States Chamber of Commerce. 1992. Winning with diversity. *Nation's Business* 80 (9).